Betty Crocker's
SOUTHWEST COOKING

▲▲▲▲▲▲▲▲▲▲

Prentice Hall

▲▲▲▲▲▲▲▲▲▲

New York   London   Toronto   Sydney   Tokyo

Prentice Hall
15 Columbus Circle
New York, New York 10023

Copyright © 1989 by General Mills, Inc., Minneapolis, Minnesota

Published simultaneously in Canada by Prentice Hall Canada, Inc.

PRENTICE HALL and colophon are registered trademarks of Simon & Schuster, Inc.

BETTY CROCKER is a registered trademark of General Mills, Inc.

Library of Congress Cataloging-in-Publication Data
Crocker, Betty.
[Southwest cooking]
Betty Crocker's Southwest cooking.—1st ed.
p.   cm.
Includes index.
ISBN 0-13-074329-1: $17.95
1. Cookery, American—Southwestern style.   2. Cookery, Mexican.
I. Title.   II. Title: Southwest cooking.
TX715.2.S69C76   1989
641.5979—dc19   88-29014
CIP

Manufactured in the United States of America

10   9   8   7   6   5   4   3   2   1

First Edition

Preceding pages:
A chili party: Texas Red Chili (page 75), White Bean
Chili (page 75) and Vegetable Cornmeal Muffins
(page 181). See page 212 for a complete chili
party menu.

A formal dinner: Spicy Pork Roast (page 120),
Spinach Budín (page 173) and Jícama Citrus Salad
with Sangria Dressing (page 169). See page 212 for a
complete formal dinner menu.

Introduction

The cuisine of the Southwest changes continuously, its evolution a result of cultural mélange and the introduction of "new" foods. It is a growing cuisine based on a brilliant variety of ingredients and native cooking techniques, and it is where the cookery of Spaniards, Mexicans and Native Americans has come together.

Southwest cooking has just recently enjoyed wide appreciation that has traveled far beyond the borders of New Mexico and Texas. Today, many of the ingredients that once were difficult to find anywhere but in the Southwest can be purchased in supermarkets across the country. What isn't to be found at the grocery store is available from Mexican specialty shops and through the dozens of mail-order houses that pepper the United States. Refer to the Glossary of Ingredients for a brief introduction to scores of typical southwestern ingredients. There you will find easy directions for such techniques as roasting tomatoes and chiles, too. And, on pages 212–213 is your key to true Southwestern Hospitality: a dozen suggestions for deliciously different, complete menus. Turn there for a guide to entertaining with flair on any occasion.

Many of the recipes in this volume are southwestern basics, featured as ingredients in other recipes. Sauces of all kinds—smooth and spicy, fresh and long-simmered—are among those basics that can be put to countless delicious uses. On pages 214–216 is a listing of those recipes that are called for as ingredients in other recipes, convenient when you are looking to satisfy a craving or looking for a way to use some extra sauce you have on hand. We hope you enjoy this introduction to southwest cooking, a glorious tradition that is the oldest, and nevertheless among the freshest and most exciting, in the land.

THE BETTY CROCKER EDITORS

Contents

Glossary of Ingredients

ACHIOTE SEED: The dried, reddish seeds of the annatto tree give food a bright orange-yellow tint when they are cooked first in hot fat; then, the seeds themselves are discarded. Sometimes they are ground to a powder and stirred into such foods as butter for color. They impart a flavor that is gentle and hard to describe; like that of saffron, it has an earthy quality.

ADOBO: A piquant sauce of tomato, vinegar and spices.

ANISE SEED: This small, elongated seed tastes sharply of licorice.

ATOLE BLUE CORNMEAL: This is blue corn that has been dried, roasted, and ground specifically to be used in making *atole*, a cornmeal gruel. Blue corn, unlike ordinary field corn, is always dried and ground before use. Cornmeal, blue, yellow or white, can be used as a thickener.

AVOCADO: This fruit is ripe when the flesh under the leathery skin yields to light pressure. A hard avocado will ripen if left at room temperature for two or three days. The Haas or California type is smaller and darker green than the emerald type grown in Florida, and some say it is more flavorful as well. Keep avocado flesh from discoloring by brushing it with lemon juice as it is peeled.

BEANS: It takes time to prepare dried beans, but the result is a tender bean that is still firm. Canned beans are sometimes mushy, but they are convenient to keep on hand and are packed in liquid that adds flavor to many recipes. Dried beans keep almost indefinitely. Before cooking dried beans, rinse them well and pick them over for stones or inferior beans.

BLACK BEANS (*frijoles negros*, turtle beans), though small, have a hearty flavor. South American cooking makes great use of them. With their dramatic dark purple-blue color, they lend themselves nicely to garnishes.

BLACK-EYED PEAS (cowpeas) are the seeds of the cowpea, an annual vine. They are tan with a blackish stain, hence "black-eyed."

GARBANZO BEANS (chickpeas) are Spanish in origin. These rounded, beige beans have a nutty flavor.

NORTHERN BEANS are white, relatively large and mild.

PINTO BEANS (*frijoles*) are charmingly speckled with brown on a pale or pinkish background.

RED BEANS are favorites in the southern states. Pinto beans may be substituted.

BUFFALO: This commercially raised red meat is lower in cholesterol and fat than beef. Unlike beef, it isn't marbled with fat. Accustomed as we are today to tender cuts of meat, buffalo is best enjoyed ground rather than as steaks.

CAPERS: These are the pickled, green buds from the prickly caper bush. They are somewhat smaller than raisins and are bottled in brine.

CAYENNE: See Chile (page 14).

CHAYOTE (christophine, mirliton, vegetable pear): Related to gourds, chayote squash have none of their brilliant decoration. Light green skin encases firm flesh of an even paler green. Chayote may be baked, steamed, stuffed and sautéed. A 1-pound chayote makes a nice serving for two or three people.

CHEESE: Traditional Mexican cheeses were made with goat's or sheep's milk. The recipes that follow use the   cheeses.

A variety of beans used in southwest cooking (clockwise from spoon): Pinto beans, black-eyed peas, red beans, garbanzo beans, black beans and great northern beans.

PLANTAIN: This relative of the banana boasts a thick skin and large size. The fruit itself tends to be a deeper yellow than that of the banana. Cooked unripe, plantain is eaten as one would a potato. Plantains are sweetest when ripe, which isn't until their skins are an alarming, thorough black. Like bananas, plantains will ripen after they have been harvested.

POSOLE: Sometimes hominy is called "posole," but the word authentically refers to a dish made with hominy as an ingredient. See Hominy, page 18.

PRICKLY PEAR: This is the diminutive (egg-size) fruit of the cactus of the same name. It is nearly impossible to avoid the prickles when peeling to reveal the garnet-colored flesh. Prickly pears are sometimes sold with the prickles removed.

PUMPKIN SEED: With the shells or husks removed, pumpkin seeds are known as *pepitas*. Store them in a cool, dry place. To toast pumpkin seeds, spread them in a single layer in an ungreased pan. Bake at 350° for 13 to 15 minutes, stirring and checking for doneness frequently.

QUAIL: These little birds usually weigh in at about ¼ pound. They have richly flavored meat, what there is of it. Quail are most commonly available frozen. See Game, page 18.

QUESO: Spanish for "cheese."

QUESO AÑEJO: The name means "aged cheese," in Spanish. See Cheese, page 14.

QUESO FRESCO: The name means "fresh cheese." See Cheese, page 14.

RABBIT: Rabbits are raised commercially. As with many uncommon meats, it is said of rabbit that it "tastes like chicken." It doesn't; it tastes like rabbit. Large rabbits aren't as tender as the little ones; it is well to marinate or stew older ones, or make rabbit sausage. See Game, page 18.

RED PEPPER: See Ground Red Pepper, page 18.

RED PEPPER SAUCE: This commercially bottled condiment is made from vinegar, spices and hot chiles. It adds heat but little in the way of flavor.

RICE: Mexican cooking calls for long-grain or medium-grain white rice. The occasional southwestern dish uses wild rice, which really isn't rice. It is the fruit of an aquatic grass once harvested only by Native Americans who lived by the Great Lakes.

SQUASH BLOSSOMS: Contrary to popular belief, the blossoms used in southwest cooking are those of winter squashes such as pumpkin, not zucchini. They are a perishable item and are best used the day they are bought.

TAMARIND: This is an intensely pungent, tart pod about four inches long. Tamarind is usually bought packaged in a tightly compressed, sticky, plastic-wrapped lump. The flesh is riddled with fibers and seeds—not what you want in your food—and must be soaked before using. Separate the tamarind pods, pulling away and discarding as much of the pod as you reasonably can. Cover with water and let the pulp soak for at least an hour (overnight, if time permits). Then, squeeze the pulp well to extract the juice, or rub as much pulp as you can through a fine-mesh sieve.

TEQUILA: A pale, sharp-tasting liquor distilled from the agave plant, which thrives in an arid, hot climate. The stem of the agave, known also as the "century plant," is used in making both *pulque* and tequila.

TOMATILLO: These fat little vegetables are the size of robust cherry tomatoes. They grow in papery husks reminiscent of Japanese lanterns and taste best when they are brilliant green in color. By the time they begin to turn yellow, they have lost some of their acid freshness. This happens when they are lightly cooked too, but then, although they relinquish their vibrant color, they develop a gentler flavor and become more luscious. Uncooked, chopped tomatillos are the basis for chunky green salsas. Select tomatillos with their husks still drawn tightly around them. Husk and rinse off the sticky residue before using them.

TOMATO: Roasting tomatoes gives them a faintly mysterious flavor. It works best with truly ripe, red tomatoes.

To roast and peel tomatoes: Set oven control to broil. Arrange cored tomatoes with their top surfaces about 5 inches from the heat. Broil, turning occasionally, until the skin is blistered and evenly browned, 5 to 8 minutes. The skins will be easy to remove. If the tomatoes are roasted on aluminum foil, clean-up will be easy and you'll be able to save any juice they give off as they roast.

TORTILLA: Tortillas are round, flat unleavened breads made from ground wheat or corn. They are the basis of Mexican cookery. Tortillas are rolled, folded, used as dippers, fried crisp and munched fresh. Corn tortillas are cut into wedges and fried for chips. For the best chips, fry tortillas that are at least one day old. Flour tortillas, softer than those made from corn, are more popular in northern Mexico where corn does not flourish; wheat was brought there by the Spanish. Commercially made tortillas of both kinds are best stored in the freezer until needed.

To soften tortillas, warm them on a hot, ungreased skillet or griddle for about 30 seconds to 1 minute. They can be warmed in a 250° oven for 15 minutes. Or, wrap several in dampened, microwavable paper toweling or microwave plastic wrap and microwave on high (100% power) for 15 to 20 seconds.

TRIPE: Usually what is meant by tripe is the lining of pig and sheep stomachs. Tripe is the identifying ingredient of traditional *menudo*, a hearty soup. Tripe needs to be thoroughly rinsed, often in three or four changes of cold water, before it can be used.

VENISON: Venison is deer meat. Because it is lean, venison needs moist heat to keep it tender. See Game, page 18.

WALNUTS: The flavor of this nut is delicious with corn. See Nuts, page 19, for toasting and grinding.

WILD RICE: See Rice, page 20.

Condiments and Sauces

Spicy, flavorful sauces and fresh relishes and salsas are essential elements of southwestern cuisine. Rarely are they mere optional features of traditional dishes. Recipes in this chapter are intended to accompany a good number of the fish, meat and tortilla dishes that follow. They are delicious with many, many more, so experiment to your heart's content. The relishes and salsas are chunky mixtures of fruits, vegetables, herbs and spices. The sauces are smoother and usually pack a punch.

A variety of southwestern sauces, shown with grilled chicken (clockwise from top): Chipotle Mayonnaise (page 28), Apricot Basting Sauce (page 29), Tomatillo Sauce (page 27), Red Pepper–Sour Cream Sauce (page 28) and Jalapeño Cream Sauce (page 28).

Appetizers, Snacks and Beverages

A profusion of appetizers is typical of the southwestern table, where a generous and colorful spread speaks of welcome and hospitality. Sometimes the difference between an appetizer and a main dish is just the size of the serving. Relishes have a place on the appetizer table, too, whether they are spread on or scooped up with crisp tortilla chips. The following pages feature dips sparked with citrus or cilantro, stuffed vegetables to nibble chilled or piping hot and classic cheese savories.

What should be drunk with southwestern food? Honest beer is often a good choice, but not the only one. Try a refreshing Southwest Smoothie (page 56) or Mexican Tea Punch (page 56), exotic Tamarind Cooler (page 55) or spicy-rich Fiesta Hot Chocolate (page 62) to accompany sweets. Here are the time-honored formulas for such traditional favorites as Sangria Blanco (page 58), Café Diablo (page 62), and the sophisticated Chartreuse Cocktail (page 58) . . . in short, a drink for every taste and every occasion.

Double Cheese Wheel

Double Cheese Wheel

1 whole, firm round Chihuahua cheese or Monterey
* Jack cheese (1 pound)*
1 package (3 ounces) cream cheese, softened
¼ cup chopped marinated artichoke hearts, drained
¼ cup pine nuts (1 ounce), toasted (page 19)
1½ teaspoons snipped fresh basil leaves or ½ teaspoon
* dried basil leaves*

Remove any wax coating or rind from Chihuahua cheese. Hollow out cheese with knife or spoon, leaving a shell ½-inch thick on side and bottom; reserve cheese shell. Finely chop enough of the scooped-out cheese to measure 1 cup (reserve any extra for another use).

Place 1 cup chopped cheese, the cream cheese, artichoke hearts, 3 tablespoons of the pine nuts and the basil in food processor workbowl fitted with steel blade; cover and process until well mixed.

Pack mixture into cheese shell. Sprinkle with remaining 1 tablespoon pine nuts; press lightly. Cover and refrigerate until filling is firm, about 3 hours.

Cut into thin wedges. Serve with assorted crackers if desired.

24 SERVINGS

Bean and Garlic Dip

2 cups Pinto Beans (page 12)
¼ cup mayonnaise or salad dressing
1 clove garlic, finely chopped
1½ teaspoons ground red chiles
¼ teaspoon salt
Dash of pepper

Mix all ingredients. Cover and refrigerate 1 hour. Serve with tortilla chips.

ABOUT 2 CUPS DIP

Corn and Walnut Dip

2 packages (8 ounces each) cream cheese, softened
¼ cup vegetable oil
¼ cup lime juice
1 tablespoon ground red chiles
1 tablespoon ground cumin
½ teaspoon salt
Dash of pepper
1 can (8¾ ounces) whole kernel corn, drained
1 cup chopped walnuts
1 small onion, chopped (about ¼ cup)

Beat all ingredients except corn, walnuts and onion in large bowl on medium speed until smooth. Stir in corn, walnuts and onion. Serve with tortilla chips.

4 CUPS DIP

Avocado and Raisin Dip

Raisins give deep background flavor to the light, fruity avocado. Fresh lime juice does more than add a sharp note of citrus; it keeps the dip fresh looking, even at room temperature.

2 avocados, peeled and chopped
½ cup raisins
½ cup vegetable oil
¼ cup lime juice
1 teaspoon sugar
1 teaspoon salt
¼ teaspoon freshly ground pepper

Place all ingredients in blender container. Cover and blend on high speed until smooth, about 45 seconds. Serve with raw vegetables, assorted crackers or fried tortillas.

1⅔ CUPS DIP

Corn and Walnut Dip

Cheese Chiles

This spicy appetizer is strictly for fun. Shredded chile-spiked cheese is molded into chile shapes, complete with cilantro stalks to imitate chile stems. Cheese Chiles can be prepared several days ahead of time; replace the cilantro "stems" before serving.

1 cup shredded Cheddar cheese (4 ounces)
1 cup shredded Colby cheese (4 ounces)
1 teaspoon ground red chiles
1 bunch cilantro stems, cut into ½-inch pieces
Paprika

Place all ingredients except cilantro and paprika in food processor workbowl fitted with steel blade; cover and process until smooth, about 1 minute. Roll mixture by teaspoonfuls into chile shapes.

Insert cilantro pieces in wide ends of shapes for stems. Sprinkle with paprika. Cover and refrigerate until serving time.

48 APPETIZERS

Nachos

Vegetable oil
6 flour or corn tortillas (6 to 8 inches in diameter)
1½ cups shredded Cheddar cheese (6 ounces)
6 jalapeño chiles, seeded and each cut into 6 strips

Heat oil (½ inch) to 365° in 8- to 10-inch skillet. Cook tortillas, one at a time, in oil: hold tortilla down in oil with tongs until light brown, about 1 minute; drain.

Place tortillas on ungreased cookie sheet. Sprinkle each with ¼ cup of the cheese. Arrange chile strips on cheese.

Set oven control to broil. Broil tortillas with tops 3 to 4 inches from heat until cheese is melted. Cut each tortilla into 6 wedges.

36 NACHOS

Cheese Chiles

Jícama Appetizer

1 jícama (about 2 pounds)
¼ cup lemon juice
1 teaspoon salt
1 teaspoon ground red chiles

Pare jícama; cut into fourths. Cut each fourth into ¼-inch slices. Arrange slices on serving plate. Drizzle with lemon juice; sprinkle with salt and ground red chiles. Refrigerate until chilled, at least 2 hours.

ABOUT 3½ DOZEN APPETIZERS

Breaded Plantain Rounds

Use only fully ripe plantains for this appetizer. To ripen plantains, store them at room temperature until their skins are black and they give slightly when gently pressed. A ripe plantain isn't as soft as a ripe banana (but it shouldn't be hard, either).

¼ cup margarine or butter
1 tablespoon lemon juice
⅓ cup fine dry bread crumbs
⅓ cup freshly grated queso añejo or Parmesan cheese
½ teaspoon ground red chiles
⅛ teaspoon pepper
2 ripe plantains, peeled and cut into ½-inch slices

Heat oven to 375°. Heat margarine and lemon juice until margarine is melted. Mix together remaining ingredients except plantains. Dip plantain slices into margarine mixture; coat with crumb mixture.

Place on greased cookie sheet. Carefully spoon any remaining margarine mixture over slices. Bake until tender and golden brown, 20 to 25 minutes.

ABOUT 30 APPETIZERS

Plantain Chips

Vegetable oil
4 plantains, cut into ¼-inch slices
1 tablespoon chile powder
½ teaspoon salt

Heat oil (1 inch) to 350° in 3-quart saucepan or 4-quart Dutch oven. Fry plantains in oil, turning once, until golden brown, about 2 minutes; drain. Toss with chile powder and salt.

ABOUT 5 CUPS CHIPS

Stuffed Mushrooms

24 medium mushrooms
2 tablespoons margarine or butter
1 medium onion, chopped (about ¼ cup)
2 tablespoons dry white wine
¼ cup dry bread crumbs
¼ cup finely chopped fully cooked smoked ham
2 tablespoons snipped parsley
1 tablespoon lime juice
1 clove garlic, finely chopped
1 teaspoon dried oregano leaves
Dash of pepper
½ cup finely shredded Monterey Jack cheese (2 ounces)

Cut stems from mushrooms; finely chop enough stems to measure ¼ cup. Heat margarine in 10-inch skillet just until bubbly. Place mushroom caps, top sides down, in margarine. Cook uncovered until mushrooms are light brown; remove mushrooms with slotted spoon.

Cook and stir onion in same skillet until tender; stir in wine. Simmer uncovered 2 minutes. Mix in chopped mushroom stems and remaining ingredients except cheese and mushroom caps; cool slightly.

Shape mixture into 24 small balls; place 1 in each mushroom cap. Sprinkle with cheese. Set oven control to broil. Place mushrooms caps on rack in broiler pan. Broil with tops 3 to 4 inches from heat until cheese is melted, about 3 minutes.

24 APPETIZERS

Bell Pepper Rajas

Rajas ("strips") usually refers to ribbons of chiles. To prepare *rajas* in the microwave oven, arrange strips on a microwave-safe serving plate. Sprinkle with toppings and cover loosely with waxed paper. Microwave on high (100% power) 1 minute; rotate plate one quarter turn. Microwave 30 to 60 seconds longer, until the cheese has melted.

½ green bell pepper, seeded and cut into 6 strips
½ red bell pepper, seeded and cut into 6 strips
½ yellow bell pepper, seeded and cut into 6 strips
¾ cup shredded Monterey Jack cheese (3 ounces)
2 tablespoons chopped ripe olives
¼ teaspoon crushed red pepper

Cut bell pepper strips crosswise into halves. Arrange in ungreased broilerproof pie pan, 9 x 1¼ inches, or round pan, 9 x 2 inches. Sprinkle with cheese, olives and red pepper.

Set oven control to broil. Broil peppers with tops 3 to 4 inches from heat until cheese is melted, about 3 minutes.

6 SERVINGS

Avocado Toast

½ cup margarine or butter, softened
½ cup mashed avocado
2 teaspoons lime juice
1½ teaspoons snipped fresh oregano leaves or
  ½ teaspoon dried oregano leaves
1 clove garlic, finely chopped
12 slices French bread, cut diagonally ½ inch thick

Beat all ingredients except bread on medium speed until smooth. Set oven control to broil. Place bread on ungreased cookie sheet. Broil with tops about 4 inches from heat until light brown, 2 to 3 minutes.

Spread each slice bread generously with avocado mixture. Broil until bubbly, about 2 minutes.

12 SERVINGS

Snappy Stuffed Tomatillos

20 tomatillos or cherry tomatoes (1¼ to 1½ inches)
⅔ cup shredded Cheddar cheese
½ cup whole kernel corn
2 packages (3 ounces each) cream cheese, softened
2 green onions (with tops), sliced
1 teaspoon ground red chiles
Ground red chiles

Cut thin slice from stem ends of tomatillos. Remove pulp and seeds with melon baller or small spoon.

Mix Cheddar cheese, corn, cream cheese, onions and 1 teaspoon ground red chiles. Fill tomatillos with cheese mixture; sprinkle with ground red chiles. Cover and refrigerate until serving time.

20 APPETIZERS

Corn and Onion Fritters

1 large onion, chopped (about 1 cup)
2 tablespoons margarine or butter
1 can (16½ ounces) whole kernel corn, drained
1 jar (4 ounces) chopped pimientos, drained
¾ teaspoon salt
¼ teaspoon pepper
Vegetable oil
1 cup all-purpose flour
½ cup shredded Colby cheese (2 ounces)
1 teaspoon baking powder
½ cup milk
2 eggs, separated

Cook and stir onion in margarine until tender. Stir in corn, pimiento, salt and pepper; cool.

Heat oil (1 inch) to 375° in 4-quart Dutch oven. Mix corn mixture, flour, cheese and baking powder. Stir in milk and egg yolks. Beat egg whites in small bowl until stiff but not dry. Fold corn mixture into egg whites.

Drop batter by rounded teaspoonfuls into oil. Fry until golden brown, turning once, about 1 minute; drain.

ABOUT 48 FRITTERS

Flautas

1 cup finely chopped cooked chicken
12 flour tortillas (7 to 8 inches in diameter)
Vegetable oil

Spoon 1 rounded tablespoon of the chicken across bottom of each tortilla. Roll up tightly; secure with wooden picks.

Heat oil (1 inch) to 350° in 4-quart Dutch oven. Cook tortillas in oil, turning once, until golden brown, about 2 minutes; drain. Remove wooden picks. Serve with Southwest Guacamole (page 38) or a salsa.

12 FLAUTAS

Blue Cornmeal Chicken Wings

¼ cup lime juice
¼ cup vegetable oil
½ teaspoon crushed red pepper
10 chicken wings (about 2 pounds)
2 tablespoons margarine or butter
½ cup blue or yellow cornmeal
2 tablespoons all-purpose flour
½ teaspoon salt
½ teaspoon ground cumin
⅛ teaspoon pepper

Mix lime juice, oil and red pepper in large glass or plastic bowl. Cut each chicken wing at joints to make 3 pieces; discard tip. Cut off and discard excess skin. Place wings in oil mixture; stir to coat. Cover and refrigerate at least 3 hours, stirring occasionally; drain.

Heat oven to 425°. Heat margarine in rectangular pan, 13 x 9 x 2 inches, in oven until melted. Shake remaining ingredients in plastic bag, or mix in bowl. Shake wings in cornmeal mixture to coat; place in pan. Bake uncovered 20 minutes; turn. Bake until golden brown, 20 to 25 minutes longer.

20 APPETIZERS

Soups and Stews

Generally speaking, southwestern soups are hearty. There is little place here for the likes of a thin broth with lonely snips of vegetable set adrift. Much more typical are Southwest Black Bean Soup with ham (page 66) and silky Butternut Squash Soup (page 68). Chicken Tortilla Soup (page 68) indeed has a base of chicken broth, but it is thick with sweet bell pepper, chunks of avocado and chicken and quickly fried strips of flour tortillas. As for stews, Beef and Tequila Stew (page 76), White Bean Chili (page 75) and Pork Stew with Corn Bread Topping (page 76) are practically meals in themselves. Warm a stack of tortillas, corn muffins or a crusty loaf of bread to serve with any of these soups and stews for a substantial lunch or simple supper.

Posole

Chicken Tortilla Soup

Based on the traditional Mexican soup *sopa az-teca*, this rich broth features crisp fried tortilla strips and creamy slices of avocado.

1 medium onion, finely chopped (about 1/2 cup)
1 clove garlic, finely chopped
2 tablespoons vegetable oil
4 cups chicken broth
1/4 cup chopped red bell pepper
1 teaspoon ground red chiles
3/4 teaspoon dried basil leaves
1/2 teaspoon salt
1/4 teaspoon pepper
1 can (15 ounces) tomato purée
1/2 cup vegetable oil
10 corn tortillas (6 inches in diameter), cut into 1/2-inch strips
2 cups cut-up cooked chicken breasts
Shredded Monterey Jack or Chihuahua cheese
Avocado slices

Cook and stir onion and garlic in 2 tablespoons oil in 4-quart Dutch oven until onion is tender. Stir in broth, bell pepper, ground red chiles, basil, salt, pepper and tomato puree. Heat to boiling; reduce heat. Simmer uncovered 30 minutes.

Heat 1/2 cup oil in 10-inch skillet until hot. Cook tortilla strips in oil until light golden brown, 30 to 60 seconds; drain. Divide tortilla strips and chicken among 6 bowls; pour broth over chicken. Top with cheese and avocado slices.

6 SERVINGS (ABOUT 1 1/2 CUPS EACH)

Butternut Squash Soup

1 medium onion, chopped (about 1/2 cup)
2 tablespoons margarine or butter
2 cups chicken broth
1 pound butternut squash, pared, seeded and cut into 1-inch cubes
2 pears, pared and sliced
1 teaspoon snipped fresh thyme leaves
1/4 teaspoon salt
1/4 teaspoon white pepper
1/4 teaspoon ground coriander
1 cup whipping cream
1 unpared pear, sliced
1/2 cup chopped pecans, toasted (page 19)

Cook and stir onion in margarine in 4-quart Dutch oven until tender. Stir in broth, squash, 2 sliced pears, thyme, salt, white pepper and coriander. Heat to boiling; reduce heat. Cover and simmer until squash is tender, 10 to 15 minutes.

Pour about half of the soup into food processor workbowl fitted with steel blade or into blender container; cover and process until smooth. Repeat with remaining soup. Return to Dutch oven; stir in whipping cream. Heat, stirring frequently, until hot. Serve with sliced pear and pecans.

6 SERVINGS (ABOUT 1 CUP EACH)

Butternut Squash Soup

Gazpacho

1 can (28 ounces) whole tomatoes, undrained
1 cup finely chopped green bell pepper
1 cup finely chopped cucumber
1 cup croutons
1 medium onion, chopped (about ½ cup)
2 tablespoons white wine
2 tablespoons olive or vegetable oil
1 tablespoon ground cumin
1 tablespoon vinegar
½ teaspoon salt
¼ teaspoon pepper

Place tomatoes, ½ cup each of the bell pepper, cucumber and croutons, ¼ cup of the onion, the wine, oil, cumin, vinegar, salt and pepper in blender container or food processor workbowl fitted with steel blade.

Cover and blend on medium speed until smooth. Cover and refrigerate at least 1 hour. Serve with remaining ingredients as accompaniments.

8 SERVINGS (ABOUT ½ CUP EACH)

Avocado Soup

3 cups chicken broth
1 cup half-and-half
1 tablespoon chopped onion
¾ teaspoon salt
¼ teaspoon snipped fresh cilantro
Dash of pepper
2 large avocados, peeled and cut up
1 clove garlic, crushed

Place 1½ cups of the broth and the remaining ingredients in blender container or food processor workbowl fitted with steel blade. Cover and process on medium speed until smooth. Stir in remaining broth.

Cover and refrigerate until chilled, about 2 hours. Garnish with sour cream and paprika or avocado slices if desired.

6 SERVINGS (ABOUT ¾ CUP EACH)

Santa Fe Melon Soup

1 large cantaloupe (about 4 pounds), pared, seeded and chopped
3 tablespoons sugar
2 tablespoons snipped fresh mint leaves
½ cup dairy sour cream
¼ cup dry white wine
2 teaspoons grated orange peel
Fresh mint leaves

Place cantaloupe, sugar and 2 tablespoons mint in food processor workbowl fitted with steel blade or in blender container; cover and process until smooth. Stir in sour cream, wine and orange peel. Garnish with mint leaves.

6 SERVINGS (ABOUT ⅔ CUP EACH)

Santa Fe Melon Soup

White Bean Chili

1 large onion, chopped (about 1 cup)
1 clove garlic, finely chopped
¼ cup margarine or butter
4 cups ½-inch cubes cooked chicken
3 cups chicken broth
2 tablespoons snipped fresh cilantro
1 tablespoon dried basil leaves
2 teaspoons ground red chiles
¼ teaspoon ground cloves
2 cans (16 ounces each) great northern beans
1 medium tomato, chopped (about ¾ cup)
Blue or yellow corn tortilla chips

Cook and stir onion and garlic in margarine in 4-quart Dutch oven until onion is tender. Stir in remaining ingredients except chopped tomato and tortilla chips.

Heat to boiling; reduce heat. Cover and simmer 1 hour, stirring occasionally. Serve with tomato and tortilla chips.

6 SERVINGS (ABOUT 1½ CUPS EACH)

Texas Red Chili

3 pounds beef boneless round steak, cut into 1-inch
   cubes
1 large onion, finely chopped (about 1 cup)
4 cloves garlic, finely chopped
¼ cup vegetable oil
2 cups tomato purée
2 to 3 tablespoons ground red chiles
1 teaspoon cumin seed, ground
1 teaspoon ground coriander
4 Anaheim chiles, seeded and chopped
4 jalapeño chiles, seeded and chopped
Shredded Cheddar cheese
Flour tortillas
Cooked pinto beans

Cook and stir beef, onion and garlic in oil in 4-quart Dutch oven until beef is brown. Stir in remaining ingredients except cheese, tortillas and beans.

Heat to boiling; reduce heat. Cover and simmer, stirring occasionally, until beef is tender, about 2 hours. Serve with cheese, tortillas and beans.

6 SERVINGS (ABOUT 1¼ CUPS EACH)

Green Chile Stew

Substitute Anaheim chiles for the poblano chiles to moderate the "heat" of the dish. This is a very fragrant stew, rich with the flavor of lamb and the accents of lemon peel and juniper berries.

3 pounds lamb boneless shoulder
1 large onion, chopped (about 1 cup)
3 cloves garlic, finely chopped
¼ cup vegetable oil
2 cups chicken broth
1 teaspoon salt
1 teaspoon dried juniper berries, crushed
¾ teaspoon pepper
1 tablespoon all-purpose flour
¼ cup water
4 medium poblano chiles, roasted, peeled (page 15),
   seeded and cut into 2 x ¼-inch strips
2 tablespoons finely shredded lemon peel

Trim excess fat from lamb shoulder; cut lamb into 1-inch cubes. Cook and stir lamb, onion and garlic in oil in 4-quart Dutch oven until lamb is no longer pink; drain.

Stir in broth, salt, juniper berries and pepper. Heat to boiling; reduce heat. Cover and simmer, stirring occasionally, until lamb is tender, about 1 hour.

Shake flour and water in tightly covered container; stir into lamb mixture. Heat to boiling, stirring constantly. Boil and stir 1 minute. Stir in chiles. Sprinkle each serving with lemon peel.

4 SERVINGS (ABOUT 1¼ CUPS EACH)

Green Chile Stew

Pork Stew with Corn Bread Topping

1 small red bell pepper
1 small yellow bell pepper
1 pound pork boneless loin, cut into 1-inch cubes
1/2 pound bulk chorizo sausage
1 large onion, chopped (about 1 cup)
2 cloves garlic, finely chopped
1 cup beef broth
1 tablespoon dried basil leaves
1 tablespoon dried cilantro leaves
2 teaspoons ground red chiles
1 cup whole kernel corn
1 medium tomato, chopped (about 1 cup)
1 small butternut or acorn squash, pared and cut into
   1/2-inch cubes (about 1 cup)
1 can (2 1/4 ounces) sliced ripe olives, drained (about
   1/2 cup)
Corn Bread Topping (right)
Fresh Tomato Salsa (page 24)

Cut 5 thin slices from each bell pepper; reserve slices. Chop remaining bell peppers (about 1/2 cup each). Cook pork, sausage, onion and garlic in 4-quart Dutch oven over medium heat, stirring occasionally, until pork is no longer pink; drain. Stir in chopped bell peppers, broth, basil, cilantro and ground red chiles. Heat to boiling; reduce heat. Cover and simmer 30 minutes, stirring occasionally. Stir corn, tomato, squash and olives into meat mixture; cook 15 minutes longer.

Heat oven to 425°. Prepare Corn Bread Topping. Pour meat mixture into ungreased rectangular baking dish, 13 x 9 x 2 inches, or 3-quart shallow casserole. Pour Corn Bread Topping over meat mixture; carefully spread to cover, sealing to edge of dish. Arrange reserved bell pepper slices on top. Bake until topping is golden brown, 15 to 20 minutes. Serve with Fresh Tomato Salsa.

8 SERVINGS (ABOUT 1 1/2 CUPS EACH)

CORN BREAD TOPPING

1 1/2 cups yellow cornmeal
1/2 cup all-purpose flour
1 cup dairy sour cream
2/3 cup milk
1/4 cup vegetable oil
2 teaspoons baking powder
1/2 teaspoon baking soda
1/2 teaspoon salt
1 egg

Mix all ingredients; beat vigorously 30 seconds.

Beef and Tequila Stew

2 pounds beef boneless chuck, tip or round, cut into
   1-inch cubes
1/4 cup all-purpose flour
1/4 cup vegetable oil
1 medium onion, chopped (about 1/2 cup)
2 slices bacon, cut up
1/4 cup chopped carrot
1/4 cup chopped celery
1/4 cup tequila
3/4 cup tomato juice
2 tablespoons snipped fresh cilantro
1 1/2 teaspoons salt
1 can (15 ounces) garbanzo beans
4 medium tomatoes, chopped (about 4 cups)
2 cloves garlic, finely chopped

Coat beef with flour. Heat oil in 10-inch skillet until hot. Cook and stir beef in oil over medium heat until brown. Remove beef with slotted spoon and drain. Cook and stir onion and bacon in same skillet until bacon is crisp.

Stir in beef and remaining ingredients. Heat to boiling; reduce heat. Cover and simmer until beef is tender, about 1 hour.

6 SERVINGS (ABOUT 1 CUP EACH)

Pork Stew with Corn Bread Topping (shown with Fresh Tomato Salsa, page 24)

Zuni Vegetable Stew

The Zuni, a tribe of Pueblo Indians, live in New Mexico. The fresh ingredients that make up this hearty stew (various chiles and squashes, corn and beans) are representative of that region's native bounty. Hot Navajo Fry Breads (page 163) would be delicious served with this one.

¾ cup chopped onion
1 clove garlic, finely chopped
2 tablespoons vegetable oil
1 large red bell pepper, cut into 2 x ½-inch strips
2 medium poblano or Anaheim chiles, seeded and cut into 2 x ½-inch strips
1 jalapeño chile, seeded and chopped
1 cup cubed Hubbard or acorn squash (about ½ pound)
2 cans (14½ ounces each) chicken broth
½ teaspoon salt
½ teaspoon pepper
½ teaspoon ground coriander
1 cup thinly sliced zucchini
1 cup thinly sliced yellow squash
1 can (17 ounces) whole kernel corn, drained
1 can (16 ounces) pinto beans, drained

Cook and stir onion and garlic in oil in 4-quart Dutch oven over medium heat until onion is tender. Stir in bell pepper, poblano and jalapeño chiles. Cook 15 minutes.

Stir in Hubbard squash, broth, salt, pepper and coriander. Heat to boiling; reduce heat. Cover and simmer until squash is tender, about 15 minutes. Stir in remaining ingredients. Cook uncovered, stirring occasionally, until zucchini is tender, about 10 minutes.

6 SERVINGS (ABOUT 1⅓ CUPS EACH)

Menudo

This is a filling soup traditionally stewed all day long, often with beef shanks or veal bones, always with tripe. Robust versions tend to include some corn, whether in hominy form or as *nixtamal* (partially cooked, dried corn). *Menudo* is informal fiesta fare.

2 pounds honeycomb tripe
4 whole cloves
1 medium onion, cut into fourths
3 cups chicken broth
2 cups water
½ cup chopped carrot
½ cup chopped celery
1 can (16 ounces) whole tomatoes, undrained
3 cloves garlic, finely chopped
1 teaspoon salt
½ teaspoon ground oregano
½ teaspoon ground sage
½ teaspoon pepper
1 tablespoon olive or vegetable oil

Rinse tripe under cold running water. Place tripe and enough water to cover in 4-quart Dutch oven. Let stand 2 hours; drain and repeat. Cut tripe into strips, 2 x ¼ inches.

Insert 1 clove into each onion fourth. Heat tripe, onion and remaining ingredients except oil to boiling; reduce heat. Cover and simmer until tripe is tender, about 4 hours. Stir in oil. Sprinkle with finely chopped green onions and snipped cilantro if desired.

8 SERVINGS (ABOUT 1 CUP EACH)

Zuni Vegetable Stew

Tortilla and Masa Specialties

These are the dishes that most characteristically represent the cooking of the Southwest. Tortillas, made with corn or flour, are the basis of the southwestern meal. They are served as bread, of course, but beyond that they are the definitive ingredient in each of the following dishes:

- A *burrito* is a flour tortilla folded like an envelope around a filling.
- *Chilaquiles* is a casserole of fried tortilla strips baked with sauces and fillings.
- A *chimichanga* is a *burrito* that traditionally is deep-fat fried after it has been filled.
- An *enchilada* is a filled corn tortilla served with a sauce.
- *Fajitas* are flour tortillas filled with slices of steak and various condiments.
- A *flauta* ("flute") is a very tightly rolled *enchilada*.
- *Nachos* are crisp chips of corn tortillas served with cheese and salsa or chiles, usually as an appetizer (page 41).
- A *quesadilla* is a tortilla, filled principally with cheese, then folded or stacked.
- And, a *taco* is a tortilla, crisp or soft, folded in half around a filling.

Masa dishes are made with cornmeal. Some contemporary *masa* recipes included here are Shrimp with Cornmeal Pancakes, (page 96), Southwest Torte (page 100) and a spectacular, simplified tamale: Turkey Tamale Pie (page 90).

Stacked New Mexico Quesadilla (shown with sour cream and Fresh Tomato Salsa, page 24)

Baked Chimichangas

Chimichangas, traditionally fried, have a tempting, even, golden brown color. The *picadillo* filling combines warm spices, nuts and dried fruits.

Almond Red Sauce (page 25)
Jalapeño Cream Sauce (page 28)
1 pound ground beef
1 small onion, finely chopped (about ¼ cup)
1 clove garlic, finely chopped
¼ cup slivered almonds
¼ cup raisins
1 tablespoon red wine vinegar
1 teaspoon ground red chiles
½ teaspoon salt
¼ teaspoon ground cinnamon
⅛ teaspoon ground cloves
1 can (4 ounces) chopped green chiles
1 medium tomato, chopped (about 1 cup)
8 flour tortillas (10 inches in diameter), warmed
1 egg, beaten
2 tablespoons margarine or butter, softened

Prepare Almond Red Sauce and Jalapeño Cream Sauce; reserve. Cook and stir ground beef, onion and garlic in 10-inch skillet over medium heat until beef is brown; drain.

Stir in remaining ingredients except tortillas, egg and margarine. Heat to boiling; reduce heat. Simmer uncovered 20 minutes; stir occasionally.

Heat oven to 500°. Spoon about ½ cup beef mixture onto center of each tortilla. Fold one end of tortilla up about 1 inch over beef mixture; fold right and left sides over folded end, overlapping. Fold remaining end down; brush edges with egg to seal. Brush each chimichanga with margarine.

Place seam sides down in ungreased jelly roll pan, 15½ x 10½ x 1 inch. Bake until tortillas begin to brown and filling is hot, 8 to 10 minutes. Serve with Almond Red Sauce and Jalapeño Cream Sauce.

4 SERVINGS

Fried Chimichangas (shown with Almond Red Sauce, page 25, and Jalapeño Cream Sauce, page 28)

Fried Chimichangas: Omit 2 tablespoons margarine or butter. Heat vegetable oil (about 1 inch) to 365°. Fry chimichangas, 2 or 3 at a time, in oil, turning once, until golden brown, 3 to 4 minutes. Keep warm in 300° oven.

Fold up 1 end of tortilla about 1 inch over beef mixture.

Fold right and left sides over folded end, overlapping.

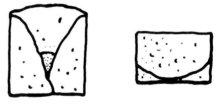

Fold down remaining end.

Beef Burritos

2 cups shredded cooked beef
1 cup Refried Beans (page 152)
8 flour tortillas (about 10 inches in diameter), warmed
2 cups shredded lettuce
2 medium tomatoes, chopped (about 2 cups)
1 cup shredded Cheddar cheese (4 ounces)

Heat beef and Refried Beans separately. Place about ¼ cup of the beef on center of each tortilla. Spoon about 2 tablespoons beans onto beef. Top with ¼ cup of the lettuce and about 2 tablespoons each of the tomatoes and cheese.

Fold one end of tortilla up about 1 inch over filling; fold right and left sides over folded end, overlapping. Fold down remaining end.

8 SERVINGS

Soft Tacos

Vegetable oil
12 corn tortillas (6 inches in diameter)
1½ cups shredded cooked beef, pork or chicken

Heat ⅛ inch oil in skillet until hot. Cook tortillas, one at a time, in the hot oil until soft, about 30 seconds; drain.

Spoon 2 tablespoons meat slightly below center of each tortilla. Roll tortilla over meat; secure with wooden pick.

Heat ⅛ inch oil until hot. Cook each taco in oil, turning once, until light golden brown, about 2 minutes; drain. Remove wooden picks. Garnish with 2 or 3 of the following if desired: chopped tomatoes, shredded lettuce, chopped onion, chopped green chiles, chopped avocado, shredded cheese.

6 SERVINGS

Texas Breakfast Tacos

Southwest Guacamole (page 38)
Fresh Tomato Salsa (page 24)
1 pound bulk chorizo sausage
1 large onion, finely chopped (about 1 cup)
1 medium green bell pepper, cut into strips
1 tablespoon margarine or butter
12 eggs, beaten
10 flour tortillas (7 to 8 inches in diameter), warmed
1½ cups shredded Co-Jack cheese (6 ounces)
2 tablespoons margarine or butter, melted

Prepare Southwest Guacamole and Fresh Tomato Salsa; reserve. Cook and stir sausage, onion and bell pepper in 10-inch skillet over medium heat, stirring frequently, until sausage is done, about 10 minutes; drain and reserve.

Heat 1 tablespoon margarine in skillet over medium heat until hot and bubbly. Pour eggs into skillet. As eggs begin to set at bottom and side, gently lift cooked portions with spatula so that thin, uncooked portion can flow to bottom. Avoid constant stirring. Cook until eggs are thickened throughout but still moist, about 5 minutes.

Heat oven to 450°. Spoon about ¼ cup sausage mixture onto each tortilla; top each with about ¼ cup eggs and 2 tablespoons cheese. Fold tortillas into halves. Arrange 5 assembled tacos in ungreased jelly roll pan, 15½ x 10½ x 1 inch; brush with melted margarine. Bake until light golden brown, 10 to 12 minutes. Repeat with remaining tacos. Serve with guacamole and salsa.

5 SERVINGS

Southwest Beef Fajitas

Set out the beef and tortillas together with all the condiments, and let guests roll their own *fajitas.*

Cucumber Salsa (page 24)
Southwest Relish (page 31)
Southwest Guacamole (page 38)
1 pound beef boneless top round steak, about ½ inch thick
¼ cup lime juice
2 tablespoons vegetable oil
2 teaspoons ground red chiles
2 cloves garlic, finely chopped
8 flour tortillas (10 inches in diameter), warmed

Prepare Cucumber Salsa, Southwest Relish and Southwest Guacamole; reserve. Cut beef steak diagonally across grain into thin slices, each 2 x ⅛ inch. Mix remaining ingredients except tortillas in glass or plastic bowl; stir in beef until well coated. Cover and refrigerate 1 hour.

Set oven control to broil. Place beef slices on rack in broiler pan. Broil with tops 2 to 3 inches from heat until brown, about 5 minutes.

Place ⅛ of the beef, some Cucumber Salsa, Southwest Relish and Southwest Guacamole on center of each tortilla. Fold one end of tortilla up about 1 inch over beef mixture; fold right and left sides over folded end, overlapping. Fold down remaining end. Serve with remaining salsa, relish and guacamole.

8 SERVINGS

Southwest Beef Fajitas (shown with Southwest Guacamole, page 38, Cucumber Salsa, page 24 and Southwest Relish, page 31)

Beef Tortilla Casserole

Basic Red Sauce (page 24)
Southwest Guacamole (page 38)
1/2 cup vegetable oil
10 corn tortillas (6 to 7 inches in diameter), cut into
*   2-inch-wide strips*
1 pound ground beef
2 Anaheim chiles, seeded and finely chopped
1 medium onion, chopped (about 1/2 cup)
1 can (15 ounces) pinto beans, drained
2 cups shredded Cheddar cheese (8 ounces)
Dairy sour cream

Prepare Basic Red Sauce and Southwest Guacamole; reserve. Heat oil in 10-inch skillet until hot. Cook tortilla strips in oil until light golden brown, about 1 minute; drain. Cook and stir ground beef, chiles and onion until beef is brown; drain.

Heat oven to 350°. Arrange tortilla strips in bottom of greased rectangular baking dish, 13 x 9 x 2 inches. Top with beef mixture, Basic Red Sauce, beans and cheese. Bake until hot and bubbly, 25 to 30 minutes. Serve with Southwest Guacamole and sour cream.

8 SERVINGS

Pork Carnitas

Southwest Guacamole (page 38)
4 poblano chiles, roasted, peeled (page 15) and seeded
1 medium onion, cut lengthwise into halves
1 pound pork boneless center loin roast, cut into
*   2 x 1/4-inch strips*
1 clove garlic, finely chopped
2 tablespoons vegetable oil
2 tablespoons tomato paste
1 tablespoon red wine vinegar
1/4 teaspoon salt
1/2 pound Italian plum tomatoes, finely chopped (about
*   1 1/3 cups)*
Flour or corn tortillas
Dairy sour cream

Prepare Southwest Guacamole; reserve. Cut chiles and onion halves lengthwise into 1/4-inch strips. Cook pork, chiles, onion and garlic in oil in 10-inch skillet over medium heat, stirring occasionally, until pork is no longer pink, about 12 minutes.

Stir in tomato paste, vinegar, salt and tomatoes; cook until hot. Serve with tortillas, Southwest Guacamole and sour cream.

4 SERVINGS

Grilled Pork Tacos

Papaya Relish (page 31)
1 tablespoon margarine or butter
1 pound pork boneless center loin roast, cut into
*   2 x 1/4-inch strips*
1/2 cup chopped fresh papaya
1/2 cup chopped fresh pineapple
10 flour tortillas (6 to 7 inches in diameter), warmed
1 1/2 cups shredded Monterey Jack cheese (6 ounces)
2 tablespoons margarine or butter, melted

Prepare Papaya Relish; reserve. Heat 1 tablespoon margarine in 10-inch skillet over medium heat until hot and bubbly. Cook pork in margarine, stirring occasionally, until no longer pink, about 10 minutes; drain. Stir in papaya and pineapple. Heat, stirring occasionally, until hot.

Heat oven to 425°. Spoon about 1/4 cup pork mixture onto half of each tortilla; top with about 2 tablespoons cheese. Fold tortillas into halves. Arrange five assembled tacos in ungreased jelly roll pan, 15 1/2 x 10 1/2 x 1 inch; brush with melted margarine. Bake until light golden brown, about 10 minutes. Repeat with remaining tacos. Serve with Papaya Relish and, if desired, dairy sour cream.

5 SERVINGS

Grilled Pork Tacos (shown with Papaya Relish,
page 31)

Shrimp with Cornmeal Pancakes

These buttermilk pancakes are made with crunchy cornmeal. Use blue cornmeal for a darker, more dramatic pancake. The sauce for the shrimp isn't too spicy—full of roasted chile flavor and not too hot.

3 poblano chiles, roasted, peeled (page 15) and seeded
2 medium tomatoes, roasted (page 20), peeled, cut into halves and seeded
1 medium onion, cut into fourths
1 clove garlic
1/4 cup dry white wine
1 teaspoon sugar
1/4 teaspoon salt
1/8 teaspoon ground red pepper
1/2 cup dairy sour cream
1 pound cooked medium shrimp
Cornmeal Pancakes (below)
1/2 cup shredded Monterey Jack cheese (2 ounces)

Place chiles, tomatoes, onion and garlic in food processor workbowl fitted with steel blade or in blender container; cover and process until smooth.

Pour into 2-quart saucepan; stir in wine, sugar, salt and red pepper. Heat to boiling; reduce heat to low. Cook uncovered, stirring occasionally, until thickened, about 15 minutes. Stir in sour cream and shrimp; heat just until hot. Spoon over Cornmeal Pancakes; top with cheese.

6 SERVINGS (6 OR 7 PANCAKES EACH)

CORNMEAL PANCAKES

2 eggs
1 cup yellow or blue cornmeal
1/4 cup all-purpose flour
2 cups buttermilk
1/4 cup margarine or butter, melted
2 teaspoons baking powder
1 teaspoon baking soda

Beat eggs in medium bowl until fluffy; beat in remaining ingredients just until smooth. For each pancake, pour about 2 tablespoons batter onto hot greased griddle. Cook until pancakes are dry around edges; turn and cook other sides until golden brown.

Grilled Seafood Flautas

Roasted Tomato Sauce (page 25)
1 package (8 ounces) frozen salad-style imitation crabmeat, thawed (about 1 1/2 cups)
1/2 cup sliced green onions (with tops)
1 tablespoon margarine or butter
1/2 cup dairy sour cream
1/2 cup shredded Monterey Jack cheese (2 ounces)
1 can (14 ounces) artichoke hearts, drained and cut into fourths
10 flour tortillas (7 to 8 inches in diameter), warmed
4 tablespoons margarine or butter

Prepare Roasted Tomato Sauce; reserve. Cook crabmeat and onions in 1 tablespoon margarine over medium heat, stirring frequently, until onions are tender. Mix in sour cream, cheese and artichoke hearts.

Spoon about 1/3 cup mixture onto one end of each tortilla. Roll up tightly into cylinder shape; secure with wooden picks.

Heat 2 tablespoons margarine in 10-inch skillet over medium heat until hot and bubbly. Cook 3 or 4 flautas in margarine, turning frequently, until golden brown, about 5 minutes. Keep warm in 300° oven. Repeat with remaining flautas, adding remaining margarine as needed. Serve with warm Roasted Tomato Sauce.

5 SERVINGS

Shrimp with Cornmeal Pancakes

Ricotta Cheese Enchiladas

These enchiladas are a southwestern version of manicotti. The cilantro and nut sauce is a nice counterpoint to the rich ricotta filling.

Roasted Tomato Sauce (page 25)
1 container (15 ounces) ricotta cheese
1 cup shredded Monterey Jack cheese (4 ounces)
¼ cup grated Sierra or Romano cheese (1 ounce)
2 tablespoons snipped fresh cilantro
1 small onion, finely chopped (about ¼ cup)
2 eggs
10 flour tortillas (8 inches in diameter), warmed
½ cup shredded Monterey Jack cheese (2 ounces)
Cilantro Pesto (page 28)

Prepare Roasted Tomato Sauce; reserve. Heat oven to 350°. Mix ricotta cheese, 1 cup Monterey Jack cheese, the Sierra cheese, cilantro, onion and eggs. Spoon about ⅓ cup mixture onto each tortilla; roll up. Place seam sides down in greased rectangular pan, 13 x 9 x 2 inches. Pour Roasted Tomato Sauce over top.

Bake uncovered until filling is set, about 40 minutes. Sprinkle with ½ cup Monterey Jack cheese; bake until cheese is melted, 3 to 4 minutes. Serve with Cilantro Pesto.

5 SERVINGS

Tortilla Skillet

½ cup vegetable oil
12 corn or flour tortillas (6 to 7 inches in diameter), cut into ½-inch strips
½ cup chopped green onions (with tops)
1 can (16 ounces) whole tomatoes, drained
½ teaspoon ground oregano
½ teaspoon salt
⅛ teaspoon pepper
1 cup shredded Monterey Jack cheese (4 ounces)
Dairy sour cream

Heat oil in 10-inch skillet until hot. Cook tortilla strips and onions in oil, turning occasionally, until tortillas are crisp, about 10 minutes.

Stir in tomatoes, oregano, salt and pepper. Sprinkle with cheese; heat just until cheese is melted. Serve with sour cream.

4 TO 6 SERVINGS

Pepita Vegetable Burritos

Burritos ("little burros") are a very common use of flour tortillas. Here the bundles are stuffed with garlicky, crisp-tender vegetables: broccoli, summer squash and sweet red bell pepper, and served with a rich pumpkin seed sauce.

Pumpkin Seed Sauce (page 27)
1 cup chopped broccoli
1 medium onion, finely chopped (about ½ cup)
2 cloves garlic, finely chopped
2 tablespoons vegetable oil
1 cup 2 x ¼-inch strips yellow squash
1 cup 2 x ¼-inch strips zucchini
½ cup finely chopped red bell pepper
¼ cup shelled pumpkin seeds, toasted (page 20)
1 tablespoon lemon juice
1 teaspoon ground red chiles
¼ teaspoon salt
¼ teaspoon ground cumin
6 flour tortillas (10 inches in diameter), warmed

Prepare Pumpkin Seed Sauce; reserve. Cook broccoli, onion and garlic in oil in 10-inch skillet, stirring frequently, until tender. Stir in remaining ingredients except tortillas. Cook, stirring occasionally, until squash is crisp-tender, about 2 minutes; keep warm.

Spoon about ½ cup of the vegetable mixture onto center of each tortilla. Fold one end of tortilla up about 1 inch over mixture; fold right and left sides over folded end, overlapping. Fold remaining end down. Serve with Pumpkin Seed Sauce.

6 SERVINGS

Pepita Vegetable Burrito

Poultry, Meats and Seafood

Southwest cooking has made great use of the chicken, perhaps the most versatile of birds. Game birds historically had their place too, but by the late nineteenth century wild turkeys, quail, pheasant and squab had grown somewhat scarce in the Southwest. Today farm-raised game birds are available nationwide, and because they don't have to scratch for a living, they are meatier than the wild birds.

The grasslands of the Southwest fostered a booming cattle industry. Beef, together with the sheep and pigs kept by Navajo Indians and Basque settlers, became important contributions to regional dishes. With the abundance of meat, the southwestern barbecue came into its own. Some say the word *barbecue* is derived from *barbacoa*, the Spanish translation of an Indian word meaning a cooking grill of green wood. Others insist it comes from the French expression for roasting a whole animal, *de barbe á queue*, "from beard to tail." Whatever the derivation, barbecues today feature buffalo, rabbit, venison and game birds in addition to lamb, pork and beef.

The importance of seafood in the southwestern repertory is somewhat recent, except around the Gulf of Mexico where the availability of fish has never been in question. Fish lends itself nicely to the Southwest's flamboyant flavors and uncomplicated cooking techniques.

Apricot-basted Quail

Apricot-basted Quail

Apricot Basting Sauce (page 29)
6 quail (about 6 ounces each)
6 slices bacon

Prepare Apricot Basting Sauce; reserve. Heat oven to 400°. Wrap each quail in 1 slice bacon. Place breast sides up, at least 1 inch apart, on rack in shallow roasting pan. Roast uncovered 30 minutes.

Brush generously with Apricot Basting Sauce. Roast until done, 15 to 20 minutes longer. Heat remaining sauce, and serve with quail.

4 TO 6 SERVINGS

Mexican Chicken

1 medium onion, thinly sliced
½ cup vegetable oil
12 pitted green olives
4 medium tomatoes, chopped (about 4 cups)
2 stalks celery, chopped
2 cloves garlic, finely chopped
2 bay leaves
½ cup water
2 tablespoons capers
1 tablespoon dried oregano leaves
1 teaspoon salt
¼ teaspoon pepper
6 boneless chicken breast halves
8 ounces mushrooms, sliced

Cook and stir onion in oil in 10-inch skillet until tender. Stir in remaining ingredients except chicken breasts and mushrooms. Heat to boiling; reduce heat. Simmer uncovered 30 minutes.

Place chicken, skin sides up, in single layer in skillet. Cover and cook over medium-low heat 30 minutes. Add mushrooms; cover and cook until chicken is done, about 15 minutes longer.

6 SERVINGS

Chicken Almendrado

This one-skillet version of "almond chicken" could hardly be easier. Ground almonds thicken a cinnamon-chile sauce nicely.

1 medium onion, chopped (about ½ cup)
2 tablespoons margarine or butter
1 tablespoon vegetable oil
1 cup chicken broth
¼ cup slivered almonds
1 tablespoon ground red chiles
1 teaspoon vinegar
½ teaspoon sugar
½ teaspoon ground cinnamon
4 boneless chicken breast halves
Slivered almonds

Cook and stir onion in margarine and oil in 10-inch skillet until tender. Stir in broth, ¼ cup almonds, the ground red chiles, vinegar, sugar and cinnamon. Heat to boiling; reduce heat. Simmer uncovered 10 minutes.

Spoon mixture into blender container; cover and blend on low speed until smooth, about 1 minute. Return sauce to skillet.

Dip chicken breasts into sauce to coat both sides. Place skin sides up in single layer in skillet. Heat to boiling; reduce heat. Cover and simmer until done, about 45 minutes. Serve sauce over chicken; sprinkle with almonds.

4 SERVINGS

Chicken Almendrado

Grilled Chicken Adobo

The Achiote Sauce Base (below) makes more than enough for two recipes. Store the remainder in the freezer for a shortcut Chicken Adobo another time.

10 boneless, skinless, chicken breast halves (about 3½ pounds)
¼ cup Achiote Sauce Base (below)
1 cup orange juice
2 tablespoons lemon juice
2 tablespoons vegetable oil
1 teaspoon dried basil leaves
1 teaspoon ground cinnamon
½ teaspoon salt

Place chicken breasts in shallow glass or plastic dish. Mix remaining ingredients; pour over chicken. Cover and refrigerate 2 hours.

Remove chicken from marinade; reserve marinade. Cover and grill chicken 5 to 6 inches from medium coals 10 to 20 minutes.

Turn chicken. Cover and grill, turning and brushing with marinade 2 or 3 times, until done, 10 to 20 minutes longer.

Heat remaining marinade to boiling. Boil uncovered until thickened, 8 to 10 minutes. Serve with chicken.

6 SERVINGS

ACHIOTE SAUCE BASE

⅓ cup achiote seeds (annatto seeds)
⅓ cup orange juice
⅓ cup white vinegar
1 teaspoon ground red chiles
½ teaspoon pepper
1 clove garlic

Cover achiote seeds with boiling water. Cover; let stand at least 8 hours. Drain seeds. Place seeds and remaining ingredients in food processor workbowl fitted with steel blade. Cover and process until seeds are coarsely ground; strain. Store in refrigerator up to 1 week or in freezer up to 2 months.

ABOUT ⅔ CUP SAUCE BASE

Broiled Chicken Adobo: Set oven control to broil. Remove chicken from marinade; reserve marinade. Place chicken in greased rectangular pan, 13 x 9 x 2 inches; pour half of the marinade over chicken. Broil chicken with tops about 4 inches from heat until light brown, about 10 minutes. Turn chicken; pour remaining marinade over chicken. Broil until done, about 6 minutes longer.

Chicken and Orange Salad

2 tablespoons finely chopped scallions or green onions (with tops)
2 tablespoons lime juice
¼ teaspoon salt
2 cups cut-up cooked chicken
1 cup cooked green peas
1 cup mayonnaise or salad dressing
¼ cup finely chopped carrot
¼ cup finely chopped celery
¼ cup finely snipped fresh cilantro
3 tablespoons orange juice
½ teaspoon salt
½ teaspoon ground cinnamon
¼ teaspoon freshly ground pepper
Lettuce leaves
3 oranges, pared and sectioned or unpared and cut into wedges
2 avocados, peeled and cut into wedges

Sprinkle scallions with lime juice and ¼ teaspoon salt; cover and refrigerate. Mix remaining ingredients except lettuce, oranges and avocados; cover and refrigerate at least 1 hour.

Spoon chicken mixture onto lettuce. Garnish with oranges and avocados; sprinkle with scallions.

6 SERVINGS

Chicken and Orange Salad

Chicken in Mole Sauce

Mole comes from the Aztec word *molli*, meaning a saucy dish. The best-known versions of *mole* are dark and highly spiced sauces for poultry and include unsweetened chocolate as an ingredient. The chocolate flavor is indistinct—unrecognizable to most people as chocolate—but adds a smooth, mysterious background note to *mole*.

1 dried chipotle chile
¼ cup shortening or lard
2 tablespoons ground red chiles
2 cups chicken broth
4 flour tortillas, (7 to 8 inches in diameter), cut into small pieces
¼ cup tomato sauce
1 small onion, chopped (about ¼ cup)
1 clove garlic, finely chopped
1 tablespoon raisins
1 tablespoon chopped almonds or walnuts
1 tablespoon sesame seed
1 tablespoon shelled pumpkin seeds
1 tablespoon peanut butter
1½ teaspoons sugar
1½ teaspoons ground oregano
1½ teaspoons cocoa
½ teaspoon anise seed
¼ teaspoon ground cinnamon
¼ teaspoon ground cloves
¼ teaspoon ground nutmeg
¼ teaspoon ground allspice
¼ teaspoon ground ginger
¼ teaspoon ground cumin or ½ teaspoon cumin seed
1 cup chicken broth
8 boneless chicken breast halves (about 4 pounds)

Cover chile with warm water. Let stand until softened, about 1 hour. Drain and finely chop.

Heat shortening in 3-quart saucepan over medium heat until hot. Cook and stir ground red chiles in shortening until brown (add about ¼ teaspoon water to prevent scorching if necessary); cool.

Stir in 2 cups broth. Stir in remaining ingredients except remaining 1 cup broth and the chicken.

Heat to boiling; reduce heat. Cover and simmer 30 minutes, stirring occasionally; cool.

Pour a small amount of sauce into blender container. Cover and blend on high speed until smooth. Repeat with remaining sauce.

Heat 1 cup of the sauce and the remaining broth to boiling in 12-inch skillet; reduce heat. Place chicken, skin sides up, in single layer in skillet. Cover and simmer until done, about 1 hour. Remove chicken to serving dish; keep warm. Measure cooking liquid. In skillet combine 1 cup of cooking liquid with the remaining sauce. Heat to boiling, stirring constantly; pour over chicken.

8 SERVINGS

Mexican Chicken Salad

2 cups cut-up cooked chicken
¼ cup dairy sour cream
¼ cup mayonnaise or salad dressing
¼ cup finely chopped carrot
2 tablespoons snipped fresh cilantro
2 tablespoons capers
2 tablespoons chopped pimiento
2 tablespoons lime juice
½ teaspoon ground cumin
½ teaspoon dried oregano leaves
1 small onion, chopped (about ¼ cup)
Lettuce leaves
1 avocado, peeled and cut into wedges
Paprika

Toss all ingredients except lettuce, avocado and paprika. Serve on lettuce with avocado; sprinkle with paprika.

4 SERVINGS

Santa Fe Chicken

Black Bean Relish (page 30)
8 boneless, skinless, chicken breast halves
¼ cup vegetable oil
2 tablespoons lime juice
½ teaspoon salt
¼ teaspoon pepper
2 cloves garlic, finely chopped
1 medium onion, chopped (about ½ cup)
1 can (14 ounces) artichoke hearts, drained and cut into fourths

Prepare Black Bean Relish; reserve. Place chicken breasts in shallow glass or plastic dish. Mix remaining ingredients except artichoke hearts; pour over chicken. Cover and refrigerate 1 hour.

Set oven control to broil. Remove chicken from marinade; reserve marinade. Place chicken in greased broiler pan (without rack); brush with marinade. Broil chicken with tops about 4 inches from heat until light brown, about 10 minutes.

Turn chicken; brush with marinade. Arrange artichoke hearts around chicken. Broil until chicken is done, 8 to 11 minutes longer. Serve with Black Bean Relish.

8 SERVINGS

Grilled Cornish Hens

Plum Barbecue Sauce (page 29)
3 Rock Cornish hens (about 1¼ pounds each)

Prepare Plum Barbecue Sauce; reserve. Cut hens lengthwise into halves. Place bone sides down on grill. Cover and grill 5 to 6 inches from medium coals 35 minutes.

Turn hens. Cover and grill, turning and brushing with Plum Barbecue Sauce 2 or 3 times, until done, 25 to 35 minutes longer. Heat any remaining sauce, and serve with hens.

6 SERVINGS

Roast Cornish Hens: Heat oven to 350°. Place cut hens, bone sides down, on rack in shallow roasting pan. Roast uncovered 30 minutes. Brush hens generously with Plum Barbecue Sauce. Roast uncovered, brushing hens with sauce 2 or 3 times, until done, about 45 minutes longer.

Duck with Pine Nut Wild Rice

Apricot Basting Sauce (page 29)
4½- to 5-pound duckling
Pine Nut Wild Rice (below)

Prepare Apricot Basting Sauce. Heat oven to 350°. Place duckling, breast side up, on rack in shallow roasting pan. Brush with Apricot Basting Sauce. Insert meat thermometer so tip is in thickest part of inside thigh muscle and does not touch bone. Do not add water. Do not cover.

Roast, brushing with sauce 2 or 3 times, until thermometer registers 180° to 185° or drumstick meat feels very soft when pressed between fingers, 2 to 2½ hours. Serve with Pine Nut Wild Rice.

4 SERVINGS

PINE NUT WILD RICE

½ cup uncooked wild rice
2 tablespoons sliced green onions (with tops)
1 teaspoon margarine or butter
1½ cups chicken broth
½ cup pine nuts (2 ounces), toasted (page 19)
½ cup chopped dried pears
½ cup currants

Cook and stir wild rice and onions in margarine in 2-quart heavy saucepan over medium heat until onions are tender, about 3 minutes. Stir in broth. Heat to boiling, stirring occasionally; reduce heat. Cover and simmer until wild rice is tender, 40 to 50 minutes. Stir in pine nuts, pears and currants.

Turkey with Southwest Stuffing

Turkey is a native American bird. One of its great virtues is that, with relatively little effort in preparation, it serves many. The rich corn bread stuffing boasts an untraditional, delicious combination of sage, cilantro and pecans. Chayote guarantees that it will be moist.

Southwest Stuffing (right)
10- to 12-pound turkey
Margarine or butter, melted

Prepare Southwest Stuffing. Fill wishbone area of turkey with stuffing. Fasten neck skin to back with skewer. Fold wings across back with tips touching. Fill body cavity lightly. (Do not pack—stuffing will expand.) Tuck drumsticks under band of skin at tail, or skewer to tail.

Spoon any remaining stuffing into ungreased 1-quart casserole; cover. (Refrigerate until about 30 minutes before turkey is done. Bake covered until hot, about 45 minutes.)

Heat oven to 325°. Place turkey, breast side up, on rack in shallow roasting pan. Brush with margarine. Insert meat thermometer so tip is in thickest part of inside thigh muscle or thickest part of breast meat and does not touch bone. (Tip of thermometer can be inserted in center of stuffing.) Do not add water. Do not cover. Roast until done, 3½ to 4 hours.

Place a tent of aluminum foil loosely over turkey when it begins to turn golden. After 2½ hours, cut band or remove skewer holding legs. Turkey is done when thermometer placed in thigh muscle registers 185° or drumstick meat feels very soft when pressed between fingers. (Thermometer inserted in stuffing will register 165°.)

Let stand about 20 minutes before carving. As soon as possible after serving, remove every bit of stuffing from turkey. Cool stuffing and turkey promptly; refrigerate separately, and use within 2 days.

8 TO 10 SERVINGS

SOUTHWEST STUFFING

1 cup chopped chayote (about 1 small)
4 jalapeño chiles, seeded and finely chopped
2 cloves garlic, finely chopped
1 large onion, finely chopped (about 1 cup)
1 cup margarine or butter
1 tablespoon snipped fresh cilantro
1 teaspoon salt
½ teaspoon dried thyme leaves
½ teaspoon dried sage leaves
9 cups ½-inch cubes corn bread
1 cup chopped pecans

Cook and stir chayote, chiles, garlic and onion in margarine in 10-inch skillet until chayote is tender. Stir in cilantro, salt, thyme and sage until well blended. Stir in about ⅓ of the corn bread cubes. Turn mixture into deep bowl. Add remaining corn bread cubes and the pecans; toss.

Turkey in Jalapeño Cream Sauce

Jalapeño Cream Sauce (page 28)
2 large boneless, skinless turkey breasts (about 1 pound each), each cut into 3 slices
¼ cup all-purpose flour
½ teaspoon cracked black pepper
¼ teaspoon salt
¼ cup margarine or butter

Prepare Jalapeño Cream Sauce; reserve. Flatten each turkey breast slice to ¼-inch thickness between plastic wrap or waxed paper.

Mix flour, pepper and salt. Coat turkey with flour mixture. Heat margarine in 10-inch skillet until melted. Cook turkey in margarine, turning once, until done, about 8 minutes. Serve with Jalapeño Cream Sauce.

6 SERVINGS

Turkey with Southwest Stuffing

Venison with Plum Sauce

Plum Barbecue Sauce (page 29)
6 venison steaks, 1 inch thick (about 4 ounces each)

Prepare Plum Barbecue Sauce. Set oven control to broil. Place venison steaks in greased broiler pan (without rack); spoon ½ cup of the sauce evenly over venison.

Broil venison with tops about 4 inches from heat until light brown, about 10 minutes. Turn venison; spoon ½ cup of the sauce evenly over venison. Broil until rare to medium-rare doneness, about 5 minutes longer. Heat remaining sauce, and serve with venison.

6 SERVINGS

Pheasant in Almond Red Sauce

Pheasant is a deep-flavored meat and delicious cooked simply, with a minimum of fuss. Almond Red Sauce is equally simple to prepare. It is thick with nuts, which always go well with game.

Almond Red Sauce (page 25)
2½- to 3-pound pheasant, cut up
2 tablespoons vegetable oil
½ cup chicken broth

Prepare Almond Red Sauce; reserve. Cook pheasant in oil in 10-inch skillet until light brown, 15 to 18 minutes; drain.

Stir in broth and Almond Red Sauce. Heat to boiling; reduce heat. Cover and simmer until pheasant is done, about 30 minutes longer. Skim fat from sauce.

6 SERVINGS

Spicy Brisket

Spicy Texas Barbecue Sauce (page 30)
4- to 5-pound well-trimmed beef brisket

Prepare Spicy Texas Barbecue Sauce. Heat oven to 325°. Place beef brisket in ungreased rectangular baking dish, 13 x 9 x 2 inches. Pour sauce over beef.

Cover and bake 2 hours. Turn beef over; cover and bake until tender, about 2 hours longer. Serve with warmed flour tortillas if desired.

12 SERVINGS

Broiled Steak

2 beef flank steaks (1 to 1½ pounds each)
½ cup lime juice
2 tablespoons dried oregano leaves
2 tablespoons olive or vegetable oil
2 teaspoons salt
½ teaspoon pepper
4 cloves garlic, crushed

Place beef steaks in shallow glass or plastic dish. Mix remaining ingredients; pour over beef. Cover and refrigerate at least 8 hours, turning beef occasionally.

Set oven control to broil. Place beef on rack in broiler pan. Broil with tops about 3 inches from heat until brown, about 5 minutes. Turn beef; broil 5 minutes. Cut beef diagonally across grain into thin slices. Serve with tortillas and guacamole if desired.

8 SERVINGS

Venison with Plum Sauce

Santa Fe Flank Steak

3 guajillo chiles
2 cloves garlic, finely chopped
1 tablespoon packed brown sugar
1 teaspoon dried thyme leaves
¼ teaspoon salt
¼ teaspoon freshly ground pepper
2 pounds beef flank steak

Place chiles and enough water to cover chiles in 2-quart saucepan. Heat to boiling. Boil uncovered 5 minutes; drain. Remove stems; finely chop chiles. Mix chiles and remaining ingredients except beef steak. Rub mixture on both sides of beef. Cover and refrigerate 1 hour.

Set oven control to broil. Place beef on rack in broiler pan. Broil with top about 3 inches from heat until brown, about 5 minutes. Turn beef; broil until of medium-rare doneness, 4 to 6 minutes longer. Cut beef diagonally across grain into very thin slices.

8 SERVINGS

Grilled Jalapeño Buffalo Burgers

Hot Chile Sauce (page 26)
1½ pounds ground buffalo or ground beef
1 medium onion, finely chopped (about ½ cup)
2 to 3 jalapeño chiles, seeded and finely chopped
1 clove garlic, finely chopped

Prepare Hot Chile Sauce; reserve. Mix remaining ingredients. Shape into 6 patties, each about ½ inch thick.

Brush grill with vegetable oil. Grill patties about 4 inches from medium coals, turning once, until of desired doneness, 4 to 6 minutes on each side for medium. Serve with Hot Chile Sauce.

6 SERVINGS

Broiled Jalapeño Buffalo Burgers: Set oven control to broil. Place patties on rack in broiler pan. Broil with tops about 3 inches from heat, turning once, until of desired doneness, 4 to 6 minutes on each side for medium.

Mexican Pot Roast

6-pound beef arm, blade or cross-rib pot roast
8 cloves garlic
4 slices bacon, cut into halves
2 teaspoons salt
½ teaspoon pepper
½ cup prepared mustard
¼ cup vegetable oil
½ cup chopped carrot
½ cup chopped celery
½ cup sliced mushrooms
2 tablespoons snipped fresh cilantro
1 teaspoon ground nutmeg
1 teaspoon ground thyme
2 jalapeño chiles, seeded and finely chopped
2 bay leaves
1 medium onion, chopped (about ½ cup)
1 bottle or can (12 ounces) beer

Make a 1½-inch-deep cut across beef roast. Wrap each clove garlic in 1 piece bacon; insert in cut. Sprinkle beef with salt and pepper; spread with mustard. Cover and refrigerate at least 4 hours.

Cook beef in oil in 4-quart Dutch oven over medium heat until brown. Stir in remaining ingredients. Heat to boiling; reduce heat. Cover and simmer until beef is tender, about 2½ hours.

Remove beef to warm platter. Remove bay leaves from broth. Skim fat from broth. Place 2 cups of the broth and vegetables in blender container; cover and blend on medium speed until smooth. Serve with beef.

12 SERVINGS

Santa Fe Flank Steak

Spicy Pork Roast

¼ cup sugar
1 teaspoon ground red chiles
1 teaspoon dried oregano leaves
½ teaspoon pepper
2-pound pork boneless loin roast

Mix sugar, ground red chiles, oregano and pepper; rub over pork roast. Cover and refrigerate 30 minutes.

Heat oven to 325°. Place pork, fat side up, on rack in shallow roasting pan. Insert meat thermometer so tip is in thickest part of pork and does not rest in fat. Roast uncovered until thermometer registers 170°, about 2 hours.

6 SERVINGS

Pork with Cumin

2 pounds pork boneless shoulder, cut into 1-inch cubes
¼ cup all-purpose flour
½ cup vegetable oil
1 medium onion, chopped (about ½ cup)
2 slices bacon, cut up
½ cup water
2 tablespoons orange juice
2 tablespoons lime juice
2 teaspoons instant chicken bouillon (dry)
2 teaspoons cumin seed
1 teaspoon dried oregano leaves
½ teaspoon salt
¼ teaspoon pepper
4 medium tomatoes, chopped (about 4 cups)
2 medium pared or unpared potatoes, diced
½ cup dairy sour cream

Coat pork with flour. Heat oil in 10-inch skillet until hot. Cook and stir pork in oil over medium heat until brown. Remove pork with slotted spoon; drain.

Cook and stir onion and bacon in same skillet until bacon is crisp. Stir in pork and remaining ingredients except sour cream. Heat to boiling; reduce heat. Cover and simmer until pork is done, about 45 minutes. Stir in sour cream; heat until hot.

7 SERVINGS

Pork Tenderloin in Tequila

¼ cup prepared mustard
2 pounds pork tenderloin
¼ cup vegetable oil
2 cloves garlic, cut into halves
¼ cup chopped carrot
¼ cup chopped celery
¼ cup lime juice
¼ cup tequila
1 tablespoon ground red chiles
1 teaspoon salt
1 teaspoon dried oregano leaves
1 teaspoon dried thyme leaves
¼ teaspoon pepper
4 medium tomatoes, chopped (about 4 cups)
1 small onion, chopped (about ¼ cup)
1 bay leaf
¼ cup snipped parsley

Spread mustard over pork tenderloin. Heat oil and garlic in 10-inch skillet until hot. Cook pork in oil over medium heat until brown. Remove garlic.

Stir in remaining ingredients except parsley. Heat to boiling; reduce heat. Cover and simmer until pork is done, about 30 minutes. Remove bay leaf. Sprinkle with parsley.

6 SERVINGS

Pork Tenderloin in Tequila

Pork Chops in Radish Sauce

Radish and Cilantro Relish (page 31)
2 tablespoons vegetable oil
6 pork loin or rib chops, about ¹/2 inch thick
1 teaspoon salt
¹/4 teaspoon pepper
2 medium tomatoes, chopped (about 2 cups)
Hot cooked rice

Prepare Radish and Cilantro Relish; reserve. Heat oil in 10-inch skillet until hot. Cook pork chops in oil over medium heat until brown; sprinkle with salt and pepper. Remove pork from skillet.

Cook and stir relish and tomatoes in same skillet 5 minutes. Add pork. Heat to boiling; reduce heat. Cover and simmer until pork is done, about 45 minutes. Serve with rice. Garnish with snipped fresh cilantro if desired.

6 SERVINGS

Spicy Texas Spareribs

Spicy Texas Barbecue Sauce (page 30)
4¹/2 pounds fresh pork spareribs, cut into serving
   pieces
1 lemon, sliced
1 large onion, sliced

Prepare Spicy Texas Barbecue Sauce; reserve. Heat oven to 325°. Place pork spareribs, meaty sides up, on rack in shallow roasting pan. Place lemon and onion slices on pork. Cover and bake 2 hours.

Pour 2 cups of the Spicy Texas Barbecue Sauce over pork. Bake uncovered, brushing with sauce 2 or 3 times, until done, about 2 hours longer. Heat any remaining sauce, and serve with pork.

6 SERVINGS

Citrus-marinated Pork Chops

2 dried chipotle chiles
6 pork loin or rib chops, about ¹/2 inch thick
¹/2 cup orange juice concentrate, thawed
¹/4 cup vegetable oil
¹/4 cup lemon juice
2 tablespoons grated orange peel
1 teaspoon salt
1 clove garlic
1 medium orange, cut into 6 slices

Cover chiles with warm water. Let stand until softened, about 1 hour. Drain and finely chop.

Place pork chops in shallow glass or plastic dish. Place chiles and remaining ingredients except orange in blender container. Cover and blend on low speed until smooth; pour over pork. Cover and refrigerate at least 3 hours, spooning marinade over pork occasionally.

Set oven control to broil. Remove pork from marinade; reserve marinade. Place pork on rack in broiler pan. Broil with tops 3 to 5 inches from heat until light brown, about 10 minutes.

Turn pork; brush with marinade. Broil until done, about 5 minutes longer. Garnish with orange slices.

6 SERVINGS

Citrus-marinated Pork Chops

Pecan-breaded Lamb Chops

These chops are irresistible. The mustard coating is a piquant French touch that holds the crusty nut coating in place and ensures juicy meat.

1 egg white
1 tablespoon Dijon-style mustard
1/2 cup finely chopped pecans
1/2 cup soft bread crumbs (about 1 1/3 slices bread)
1 clove garlic, finely chopped
6 lamb loin or shoulder chops, about 3/4 inch thick
2 tablespoons vegetable oil
2 tablespoons brandy

Beat egg white slightly in small bowl; stir in mustard. Mix pecans, bread crumbs and garlic. Dip lamb chops into mustard mixture; coat with pecan mixture.

Heat oil in 10-inch skillet until hot. Cook lamb in oil over low heat until deep golden brown, about 10 minutes on each side. Remove from heat; immediately sprinkle brandy around lamb in skillet.

6 SERVINGS

Baked Citrus Swordfish

Citrus Barbecue Sauce (page 29)
6 swordfish or salmon steaks, 1 inch thick (about 5 ounces each)

Prepare Citrus Barbecue Sauce. Heat oven to 450°. Place fish steaks in ungreased rectangular baking dish, 13 x 9 x 2 inches. Pour 1 cup of the sauce over fish.

Bake uncovered until fish flakes easily with fork, 20 to 25 minutes. Serve with remaining Citrus Barbecue Sauce.

6 SERVINGS

Baked Red Snapper

2 pounds red snapper fillets, cut into 8 serving pieces
1 cup milk
1 teaspoon dried oregano leaves
1 medium onion, sliced
1/4 cup olive or vegetable oil
1/2 cup pitted ripe olives
1/4 cup dry white wine
1/4 cup lemon juice
2 tablespoons capers
1 teaspoon ground cumin
1/2 teaspoon salt
1/4 teaspoon pepper
4 large tomatoes, chopped (about 4 cups)
2 cloves garlic, finely chopped

Place fish fillets in shallow glass or plastic dish. Mix milk and oregano; pour over fish. Cover and refrigerate 1 hour.

Cook and stir onion in oil in 10-inch skillet until tender. Stir in remaining ingredients except fish. Simmer uncovered until thickened, about 15 minutes.

Heat oven to 350°. Drain fish; pat dry. Place 1 piece fish on each of eight 12-inch squares heavy-duty aluminum foil. Spoon some tomato mixture onto fish. Fold foil over fish; seal securely. Place foil packets in ungreased jelly roll pan, 15 1/2 x 10 1/2 x 1 inch. Bake until fish flakes easily with fork, about 30 minutes. Serve with snipped fresh cilantro and lemon wedges if desired.

8 SERVINGS

Pecan-breaded Lamb Chops

Sea Bass in Cilantro

*2 pounds sea bass or red snapper fillets, cut into 8
   serving pieces*
1 cup milk
1 teaspoon ground cumin
1 large onion, finely chopped (about 1 cup)
¼ cup vegetable oil
1 cup finely chopped canned green chiles
¼ to ½ cup snipped fresh cilantro
¾ teaspoon salt
¼ teaspoon pepper
Lime or lemon wedges

Place fish fillets in shallow glass or plastic dish. Mix milk and cumin; pour over fish. Cover and refrigerate 1 hour.

Cook and stir onion in oil in 2-quart saucepan until tender. Stir in remaining ingredients except fish and lime wedges. Heat to boiling; reduce heat. Simmer uncovered until thickened, about 10 minutes.

Heat oven to 350°. Drain fish; pat dry. Place 1 piece fish on each of eight 12-inch squares heavy-duty aluminum foil. Spoon some onion mixture onto fish. Fold foil over fish; seal securely. Place foil packets in ungreased jelly roll pan, 15½ x 10½ x 1 inch. Bake until fish flakes easily with fork, 25 to 30 minutes. Serve with lime wedges.

8 SERVINGS

Paella-stuffed Snapper

A whole stuffed fish makes a stunning presentation, and this one feeds a crowd. Paella is a Spanish invention that combines seafood and meats with saffron-scented rice. Serrano chiles give the paella stuffing a Mexican kick.

Paella Stuffing (below)
*6- to 8-pound red snapper, cod or lake trout, cleaned
   and dressed*
Lime juice
¼ cup margarine or butter, melted
2 tablespoons lime juice
Lime wedges

Prepare Paella Stuffing. Heat oven to 350°. Rub cavity of fish with lime juice; fill with Paella Stuffing. Close opening with skewers; lace with string. Place in large ungreased broiler pan (without rack) or in shallow roasting pan.

Mix margarine and 2 tablespoons lime juice. Bake fish uncovered, brushing with margarine mixture occasionally, until fish flakes easily with fork, about 1½ hours. Serve with lime wedges.

10 SERVINGS

PAELLA STUFFING

½ pound chorizo sausage links, chopped
1 large onion, chopped (about 1 cup)
2 cloves garlic, finely chopped
2 serrano chiles, seeded and chopped
2 tablespoons margarine or butter
2 cups cooked rice
½ cup slivered almonds, toasted
¼ cup snipped fresh cilantro
¼ cup tomato sauce
¼ teaspoon ground saffron
1 package (6 ounces) frozen cooked medium shrimp

Cook sausage, onion, garlic and chiles in margarine in 10-inch skillet over medium heat, stirring frequently, until sausage is done, about 10 minutes; drain. Stir in remaining ingredients.

Paella-stuffed Snapper (shown before cooking)

Sole Steamed in Corn Husks

Chipotle Mayonnaise (page 28)
12 dried corn husks
2 poblano chiles, roasted, peeled (page 15), seeded and
*   chopped*
2 red bell peppers, chopped
1 medium tomato, seeded and chopped (about ¾ cup)
2 cloves garlic, finely chopped
¼ teaspoon salt
2 pounds sole or orange roughy fillets

Prepare Chipotle Mayonnaise; reserve. Rinse corn husks and remove silk; cover with boiling water. Let stand until softened, at least 1 hour; drain, and pat dry. Mix remaining ingredients except fish fillets and Chipotle Mayonnaise.

Cut fish into 1-inch pieces; divide evenly among corn husks. Place 2 to 3 tablespoons of the chile mixture on fish. Roll corn husks lengthwise around filling. Fold ends up toward center; secure with string.

Place corn husk packets on rack in 6-quart Dutch oven or steamer. Pour boiling water into Dutch oven to just below rack level. Cover; simmer until fish flakes easily with fork, about 25 minutes. Serve with Chipotle Mayonnaise.

6 SERVINGS

Roll corn husks lengthwise around filling.

Fold up ends toward center; secure with string.

Grilled Red Snapper with Vegetable Sauté

Southwest Vegetable Sauté (including Lime Butter
*   Sauce) (page 176)*
8 red snapper or cod fillets (about 5 ounces each)
¼ cup vegetable oil
Salt and pepper

Prepare Southwest Vegetable Sauté and Lime Butter Sauce; keep warm. Generously brush fish fillets with oil; sprinkle with salt and pepper.

Grill over medium coals until fish flakes easily with fork, 10 to 12 minutes. Serve with Southwest Vegetable Sauté and Lime Butter Sauce.

8 SERVINGS

Broiled Red Snapper: Set oven control to broil. Place fish on rack in broiler pan. Broil with tops about 4 inches from heat until fish flakes easily with fork, 10 to 12 minutes.

Cod with Garlic

2 pounds cod or scrod fillets, cut into 8 serving pieces
8 cloves garlic, finely chopped
2 tablespoons margarine or butter
2 tablespoons vegetable oil
¼ cup lemon juice
1 teaspoon salt
Snipped fresh cilantro

Place fish fillets on rack in broiler pan. Cook and stir garlic in margarine and oil until golden brown. Remove garlic; reserve. Drizzle margarine mixture and lemon juice over fish; sprinkle with salt.

Set oven control to broil. Broil fish with tops about 3 inches from heat until fish flakes easily with fork, 10 to 12 minutes. Sprinkle with garlic and cilantro. Serve with lemon wedges if desired.

8 SERVINGS

Grilled Red Snapper with Vegetable Sauté

Halibut with Cilantro Pesto

Cilantro Pesto (page 28)
6 halibut steaks, 1 inch thick (about 5 ounces each)
2 tablespoons margarine or butter, melted
2 tablespoons lemon juice

Prepare Cilantro Pesto; reserve. Heat oven to 450°. Place fish steaks in ungreased rectangular baking dish, 13 x 9 x 2 inches. Mix margarine and lemon juice; pour over fish.

Bake uncovered until fish flakes easily with fork, 20 to 25 minutes. Serve with Cilantro Pesto.

6 SERVINGS

Salmon with Cucumber Salsa

One classic sauce for poached salmon is a creamy one thick with cucumbers. Here, a livelier version benefits from the tang and reduced calories of yogurt.

Cucumber Salsa (page 24)
2 cups water
1 cup dry white wine
1 teaspoon salt
1/4 teaspoon dried thyme leaves
1/4 teaspoon dried oregano leaves
1/8 teaspoon ground red pepper
4 black peppercorns
4 cilantro sprigs
1 small onion, sliced
2 pounds salmon fillets, cut into 6 serving pieces

Prepare Cucumber Salsa; reserve. Heat remaining ingredients except fish fillets to boiling in 12-inch skillet; reduce heat. Cover and simmer 5 minutes.

Place fish in skillet; if necessary, add water so that fish is covered. Heat to boiling; reduce heat. Simmer uncovered until fish flakes easily with fork, about 14 minutes.

Carefully remove fish from skillet with slotted spatula; drain on wire rack. Cover and refrigerate until cold, about 2 hours. Serve with Cucumber Salsa.

6 SERVINGS

Salmon with Cucumber Salsa

Shrimp and Potato Salad

Cool shrimp salad is made even more refreshing with the snap of fresh lime juice and cilantro. This would be a substantial luncheon dish, doubly welcome because it can be made ahead.

2½ cups cooked small shrimp
2 cups cubed cooked potatoes
1 cup cooked green peas
¼ cup chopped celery
2 tablespoons lime juice
1 teaspoon ground cumin
¼ teaspoon salt
⅛ teaspoon freshly ground pepper
¾ cup mayonnaise or salad dressing
4 tablespoons snipped fresh cilantro
Lettuce leaves
3 tomatoes, cut into wedges

Mix shrimp, potatoes, peas, celery, lime juice, cumin, salt and pepper. Cover and refrigerate at least 2 hours.

Just before serving, toss shrimp mixture, mayonnaise and 3 tablespoons of the cilantro until potatoes are well coated. Serve on lettuce with tomatoes and remaining cilantro.

6 SERVINGS

Grilled Texas Shrimp

¼ cup vegetable oil
¼ cup tequila
¼ cup red wine vinegar
2 tablespoons lime juice
1 tablespoon ground red chiles
½ teaspoon salt
2 cloves garlic, finely chopped
1 red bell pepper, finely chopped
24 large raw shrimp, peeled and deveined (leave tails intact)

Mix all ingredients except shrimp in shallow glass or plastic dish; stir in shrimp. Cover and refrigerate 1 hour.

Remove shrimp from marinade; reserve marinade. Thread 4 shrimp on each of six 8-inch metal skewers. Grill over medium coals, turning once, until pink, 2 to 3 minutes on each side.

Heat marinade to boiling in nonaluminum saucepan; reduce heat to low. Simmer uncovered until bell pepper is tender, about 5 minutes. Serve with shrimp.

6 SERVINGS

Broiled Texas Shrimp: Set oven control to broil. Place skewered shrimp on rack in broiler pan. Broil with tops about 4 inches from heat, turning once, until pink, 2 to 3 minutes on each side.

Grilled Texas Shrimp

Shrimp Cilantro

1 medium onion, chopped (about ¹/₂ cup)
2 cloves garlic, finely chopped
2 tablespoons margarine or butter
2 tablespoons vegetable oil
16 large raw shrimp, peeled and deveined
2 tablespoons snipped fresh cilantro
Lemon slices

Cook and stir onion and garlic in margarine and oil in 10-inch skillet until tender. Add shrimp; cook 1 minute.

Turn shrimp; cook until pink, about 2 minutes longer. (Do not overcook.) Remove shrimp to serving dish; sprinkle with cilantro. Pour pan juices over shrimp; serve with lemon slices.

4 SERVINGS

Southwest Sautéed Scallops

2 cups water
1 dried Anaheim chile
¹/₄ cup sliced green onions (with tops)
2 tablespoons margarine or butter
2 tablespoons lime juice
2 pounds sea scallops
2 cups cubed fresh pineapple
1 cup Chinese pea pod halves (about 3 ounces)
3 cups hot cooked fettuccine

Heat water to boiling in 1-quart saucepan. Add chile. Boil 5 minutes; drain. Remove stem and seeds; finely chop chile.

Cook and stir onions, margarine, lime juice and chile in 10-inch skillet until margarine is melted. Carefully stir in scallops. Cook over medium heat, stirring frequently, until scallops turn white, about 12 minutes.

Stir in the pineapple and pea pods; heat until hot. Remove scallop mixture with slotted spoon; keep warm.

Heat liquid in skillet to boiling. Boil until slightly thickened and reduced by half. Spoon scallop mixture onto fettuccine; pour liquid over scallop mixture.

6 SERVINGS

Shrimp Cilantro (shown with a Margarita Sunrise, page 56)

Huevos Rancheros

Huevos Rancheros ("ranch-style eggs") in fact refers to any egg dish served on tortillas. Spicy sausage makes this version a hearty one.

8 ounces bulk chorizo sausage
Vegetable oil
6 corn tortillas (6 to 7 inches in diameter)
1¼ cups warm Casera Sauce (page 25)
6 fried eggs
1½ cups shredded Cheddar cheese (6 ounces)

Cook and stir sausage until done; drain. Heat ⅛ inch oil in 8-inch skillet over medium heat just until hot. Cook tortillas, one at a time, in oil until crisp, about 1 minute; drain.

Spread each tortilla with 1 tablespoon Casera Sauce to soften. Place 1 egg on each tortilla; top each with scant tablespoon Casera Sauce, ¼ cup sausage, another tablespoon sauce and ¼ cup cheese.

6 SERVINGS

Mexican Omelet

Casera Sauce (page 25)
2 eggs
2 tablespoons half-and-half
½ teaspoon dried oregano leaves
¼ teaspoon salt
Dash of pepper
1 tablespoon margarine or butter
¼ cup shredded Monterey Jack cheese (1 ounce)
2 tablespoons chopped green chiles
Dairy sour cream

Prepare Casera Sauce; reserve. Mix eggs, half-and-half, oregano, salt and pepper with fork just until whites and yolks are blended. Heat margarine in 8-inch skillet or omelet pan over medium-high heat. As margarine melts, tilt skillet to coat bottom completely. When margarine just begins to brown, skillet is hot enough to use.

Quickly pour egg mixture into skillet. Slide skillet back and forth rapidly over heat, and, at the same time, stir quickly with fork to spread eggs continuously over bottom of skillet as they thicken. Let stand over heat a few seconds to lightly brown bottom of omelet. (Do not overcook; omelet will continue to cook after folding.)

Tilt skillet; run fork under edge of omelet, then jerk skillet sharply to loosen eggs from bottom of skillet. Sprinkle with cheese and chiles. Fold portion of omelet nearest you just to center. (Allow for portion of omelet to slide up sides of skillet.)

Turn omelet onto warm plate, flipping folded portion of omelet over so far side is on bottom. Tuck sides of omelet under if necessary. Top with Casera Sauce and sour cream; sprinkle with snipped fresh cilantro if desired.

1 SERVING

Eggs and Chorizo

1 small onion, chopped (about ¼ cup)
2 tablespoons vegetable oil
8 ounces bulk chorizo sausage
8 eggs
¼ cup half-and-half
½ teaspoon dried oregano leaves

Cook and stir onion in oil in 10-inch skillet until tender. Add sausage; cook and stir until sausage is done; drain.

Mix eggs, half-and-half and oregano thoroughly with fork. Pour into sausage mixture in skillet. Cook over medium heat. As mixture begins to set at bottom and side, gently lift cooked portion with spatula so that thin, uncooked portion can flow to bottom. Avoid constant stirring. Cook until eggs are cooked throughout but still moist, 3 to 5 minutes.

6 SERVINGS

Mexican Omelet

Pumpkin Ravioli

1 cup ricotta cheese
½ cup canned pumpkin
½ teaspoon salt
¼ teaspoon ground nutmeg
2 cups all-purpose flour
½ teaspoon salt
¼ cup tomato paste
1 tablespoon olive or vegetable oil
2 eggs
Pumpkin Seed Sauce (page 27)

Mix cheese, pumpkin, ½ teaspoon salt and the nutmeg; reserve.

Mix flour and ½ teaspoon salt in large bowl; make well in center. Beat tomato paste, oil and eggs until well blended; pour into well. Stir with fork, gradually bringing flour mixture to center, until dough forms a ball. If dough is too dry, mix in up to 2 tablespoons water. Knead on lightly floured cloth-covered surface, adding flour if dough is sticky, until smooth and elastic, about 5 minutes. Cover; let rest 5 minutes.

Divide dough into 4 equal parts. Roll dough, one part at a time, into rectangle, about 12 x 10 inches (keep remaining dough covered). Drop pumpkin mixture by 2 level teaspoonfuls onto half of the rectangle about 1½ inches apart in 2 rows of 4 mounds each. Moisten edges of dough and dough between rows of pumpkin mixture with water. Fold other half of dough up over pumpkin mixture, pressing dough down around mixture. Trim edges with pastry wheel or knife. Cut between rows of filling to make ravioli; press edges with fork to seal. Repeat with remaining dough and pumpkin mixture. Place ravioli on towel; let stand, turning once, until dry, about 30 minutes.

Prepare Pumpkin Seed Sauce. Heat until hot; keep warm. Cook ravioli in 4 quarts boiling salted water (2 teaspoons salt) until tender, 10 to 15 minutes; drain carefully. Serve ravioli with sauce.

6 SERVINGS

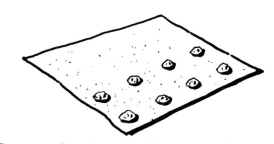

Drop pumpkin mixture by 2 level teaspoonfuls onto half of the rectangle about 1½ inches apart in 2 rows of 4 mounds each.

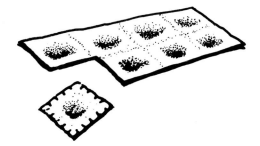

Cut between rows of filling to make ravioli; press edges with fork to seal.

Macaroni con Queso

Chile con Queso (page 38)
½ cup milk
4 ounces uncooked elbow macaroni or macaroni shells (about 1 cup)
1 large tomato, chopped (about 1 cup)
1 tablespoon snipped fresh cilantro
1 cup shredded Cheddar or Monterey Jack cheese (4 ounces)
¼ cup crushed tortilla chips

Heat oven to 375°. Prepare Chile con Queso as directed except stir in milk with the half-and-half; reserve. Cook macaroni as directed on package; drain.

Mix macaroni, Chile con Queso, tomato and cilantro in ungreased 1½-quart casserole. Sprinkle with cheese and tortilla chips. Bake uncovered until hot, about 30 minutes.

4 SERVINGS

Pumpkin Ravioli

Beans, Corn and Rice

Where would southwestern food be without beans, corn and rice? Each one of these staples was a food of the earliest inhabitants of the Southwest. The very name of the class of bean "haricot"—which includes all dried beans—comes from the Aztec word *ayacotl.* Pinto beans are the most prevalent, with red and black beans the basis of those dishes from the Sonoran and Yucatán regions of Mexico.

The gathering of corn continues to be an event celebrated by the Hopi Indians of Arizona. Traditionally the Hopis planted corn of four colors: yellow, blue, red and white. Each color represented a virtue: knowledge, patience, respect and purity respectively. Dried corn kernels thousands of years old, found in Mayan and other ruins, are testimony to the history of man's dependence on this virtually life-sustaining vegetable.

The Spanish brought rice with them to Mexico, and from there it spread throughout the Southwest. Rice is usually prepared as part of a mild dish in order to complement (and quench the fire of) hot foods. Red Rice is a rather spicy exception.

Corn-stuffed Poblano Chiles

Corn-stuffed Poblano Chiles

6 poblano chiles
2 eggs
1½ cups whole kernel corn
½ cup shredded Cheddar cheese (2 ounces)
½ cup chopped pecans
½ cup finely chopped red bell pepper
¼ cup finely chopped onion
½ teaspoon salt
⅛ teaspoon ground red pepper

Set oven control to broil. Cut chiles lengthwise into halves; carefully remove seeds. Place cut sides down on rack in broiler pan. Broil with tops about 4 inches from heat until skin blisters. Place chiles in plastic bag 15 minutes. Carefully remove as much skin as possible.

Heat oven to 375°. Beat eggs in medium bowl until thick and lemon colored, about 4 minutes; stir in remaining ingredients. Place chiles in greased rectangular baking dish, 13 x 9 x 2 inches. Spoon about ¼ cup of the corn mixture into each chile half. Cover and bake until corn mixture is hot, about 25 minutes.

6 SERVINGS

Frontier Beans

1 cup sliced green onions (with tops)
½ pound chorizo sausage links, chopped
2 cans (16 ounces each) pinto beans, 1 can drained
3 small poblano chiles, roasted, peeled, (page 15)
  seeded and chopped
1 large tomato, chopped (about 1 cup)
¼ teaspoon salt

Heat oven to 350°. Cook and stir onions and sausage until sausage is done; drain.

Mix sausage mixture and remaining ingredients in ungreased 2-quart casserole. Bake uncovered until hot and bubbly, about 30 minutes.

6 SERVINGS

Frontier Beans

Spicy Garbanzos

1 teaspoon whole mustard seed
1 medium onion, chopped (about ½ cup)
1 tablespoon vegetable oil
2 cans (15 ounces each) garbanzo beans, drained
½ cup chicken broth
2 tablespoons tomato paste
½ teaspoon salt
¼ teaspoon ground cinnamon
⅛ teaspoon ground cloves

Cook and stir mustard seed and onion in oil in 2-quart saucepan until onion is tender. Stir in remaining ingredients; cook, stirring occasionally, until beans are heated through, 5 minutes.

6 SERVINGS

Pinto Beans

Every Old West chuck wagon was outfitted with large cast-iron kettles, used to cook everything from sourdough bread to beans. Dried beans (usually pinto beans) were a cowboy's bland staple. Chiles, meats, vinegar and oftentimes beer were added to give the beans flavor.

4 cups water
1 pound dried pinto or black beans (about 2 cups)
1 medium onion, chopped (about ½ cup)
¼ cup vegetable oil
1 teaspoon salt
1 teaspoon cumin seed
2 cloves garlic, crushed
1 slice bacon

Mix water, beans and onion in 4-quart Dutch oven. Cover and heat to boiling. Boil 2 minutes. Remove from heat; let stand 1 hour.

Add just enough water to beans to cover. Stir in remaining ingredients. Heat to boiling; reduce heat. Cover and boil gently, stirring occasionally, until beans are very tender, about 2 hours (add water during cooking if necessary); drain. Beans can be covered and refrigerated up to 10 days.

ABOUT 8 SERVINGS

Corn Fritters

½ recipe Roasted Tomato Sauce (page 25)
Vegetable oil
1 cup all-purpose flour
½ cup milk
1 teaspoon baking powder
1 teaspoon vegetable oil
¼ teaspoon salt
2 eggs
1 cup whole kernel corn

Prepare Roasted Tomato Sauce; keep warm. Heat oil (1 inch) in deep fryer or 4-quart Dutch oven to 375°. Beat remaining ingredients except corn with hand beater until smooth; stir in corn.

Drop by level tablespoonfuls into hot oil. Fry until completely cooked, about 5 minutes; drain. Serve with Roasted Tomato Sauce.

9 SERVINGS

Corn Soufflé

Both this mild soufflé and the accompanying Green Chile Cheese Sauce feature a hint of cumin, the spice many associate with the flavor of the Southwest.

3 tablespoons margarine or butter
3 tablespoons all-purpose flour
¼ teaspoon sugar
¼ teaspoon ground cumin
¼ teaspoon ground nutmeg
¼ teaspoon ground red pepper
1 cup milk
3 eggs, separated
2 tablespoons finely chopped onion
2 tablespoons finely chopped green chiles
1 can (8¾ ounces) whole kernel corn, drained
Green Chile Cheese Sauce (right)

Heat oven to 350°. Butter 1-quart soufflé dish or casserole. Heat margarine in 2-quart saucepan over low heat until melted. Stir in flour, sugar, cumin, nutmeg and red pepper. Cook over low heat, stirring constantly, until mixture is smooth and bubbly. Stir in milk; heat to boiling, stirring constantly. Boil and stir 1 minute.

Beat egg yolks slightly in medium bowl. Stir at least half of the hot mixture gradually into egg yolks. Stir back into hot mixture in saucepan. Boil and stir 1 minute. Remove from heat; stir in onion, chiles and corn.

Beat egg whites in medium bowl on high speed until stiff. Stir about one-fourth of the egg whites into corn mixture. Fold corn mixture into remaining egg whites. Carefully pour mixture into soufflé dish.

Bake uncovered until knife inserted in center comes out clean, about 50 minutes. Prepare Green Chile Cheese Sauce. Serve soufflé immediately with sauce.

6 SERVINGS

GREEN CHILE CHEESE SAUCE

½ cup shredded Cheddar cheese (2 ounces)
¼ cup finely chopped green chiles
⅓ cup half-and-half
1 tablespoon finely chopped onion
1 teaspoon ground cumin
¼ teaspoon salt

Heat all ingredients over low heat, stirring constantly, until cheese is melted.

Corn Fritters with Roasted Tomato Sauce

Grilled Corn with Chile-Lime Spread

No other method of cooking can quite match the outdoors flavor of fresh corn grilled in its husk. Before it is cooked, the corn is slathered with Chile-Lime Spread.

½ cup margarine or butter, softened
½ teaspoon grated lime peel
3 tablespoons lime juice
1 to 2 teaspoons ground red chiles
6 ears corn (with husks)

Mix all ingredients except corn. Remove large outer husks from each ear corn; turn back inner husks, and remove silk. Spread each ear corn with about 2 teaspoons margarine mixture; reserve remaining margarine mixture.

Pull husks up over ears; tie with fine wire to secure. Grill corn 3 inches from medium coals, turning frequently, until done, 20 to 30 minutes. Serve with remaining margarine mixture.

6 SERVINGS

Roast Corn with Chile-Lime Spread: Heat oven to 475°. Prepare corn as directed. Roast in ungreased jelly roll pan, 15½ x 10½ x 1 inch, turning frequently, until done, 30 to 35 minutes.

Southwest Green Rice

2 large poblano chiles, roasted, peeled (page 15) and seeded
2 cloves garlic, finely chopped
1 medium onion, chopped (about ½ cup)
1 cup uncooked regular rice
2 cups chicken broth
¼ teaspoon salt
¼ cup snipped parsley

Place chiles, garlic and onion in food processor workbowl fitted with steel blade or in blender container; cover and process until smooth.

Mix chile mixture and remaining ingredients except parsley in 3-quart saucepan. Heat to boiling, stirring once or twice; reduce heat. Cover and simmer 16 minutes. (Do not lift cover or stir.) Remove from heat; fluff rice lightly with fork. Cover and let steam 10 minutes. Stir in parsley.

6 SERVINGS

Red Rice

1 large red bell pepper, roasted, peeled (page 15) and seeded
1 to 2 red jalapeño chiles, roasted, peeled (page 15) and seeded
1 small onion, chopped (about ¼ cup)
1 clove garlic, finely chopped
2 tablespoons margarine or butter
1 cup uncooked regular rice
2 cups chicken broth
¼ teaspoon salt
⅛ teaspoon red pepper sauce

Place bell pepper and chiles in food processor workbowl fitted with steel blade or in blender container; cover and process until smooth.

Cook and stir onion and garlic in margarine in 3-quart saucepan until onion is tender. Stir in remaining ingredients except bell pepper mixture. Heat to boiling, stirring once or twice; reduce heat. Cover and simmer 16 minutes. (Do not lift cover or stir.) Remove from heat; stir in bell pepper mixture. Cover and let steam 10 minutes.

6 SERVINGS

Grilled Corn with Chile-Lime Spread

Salads, Vegetables and Breads

The splendid variety of southwestern vegetables is due not only to the changing seasons, but to the patchwork of climates that covers this territory. Even semiarid ranges have, with irrigation, been coaxed into farmland. Jícama, *nopales*, chayote and of course chiles are featured in the recipes that follow, as well as the more widely familiar squashes, corn and sweet potatoes.

The truly authentic breads of the Southwest are those handed down from Native Americans. Navajo Fry Bread (page 163), Pueblo Adobe Bread (page 181), and corn breads are among them. Anise rolls (*semitas*), for example, are a New Mexican sweet bread traditionally baked to signal feast days.

Navajo Fry Bread

Navajo Fry Breads

Navajo Fry Bread is a Santa Fe specialty that has become popular throughout the Southwest. A hole is always poked through the center of each round of dough so that the bread puffs spectacularly when cooked in hot oil.

2 cups all-purpose flour
2 teaspoons baking powder
1 teaspoon salt
2 tablespoons shortening
2/3 cup warm water
Vegetable oil

Mix flour, baking powder and salt; cut in shortening until mixture resembles fine crumbs. Sprinkle in water, 1 tablespoon at a time, tossing with fork until all flour is moistened and dough almost cleans side of bowl. Gather into ball; cover and refrigerate 30 minutes.

Heat oil (1 inch) to 400° in 4-quart Dutch oven. Divide dough into 12 equal pieces. Roll each piece into 6-inch circle on lightly floured surface. Let rest a few minutes.

Make a hole about ½ inch in diameter in center of each circle. Fry circles, turning once, until puffed and golden, about 1 minute on each side; drain. Serve warm.

12 BREADS

Mexican Flag Salad

6 cups water
2 tablespoons lime juice
1 pound whole green beans
1 small jícama, pared and cut into ¼-inch strips (about 2 cups)
2 red bell peppers, cut into ¼-inch strips
Herbed Vinaigrette (below)
Lettuce leaves
6 to 8 ripe olives, finely chopped

Heat water and lime juice to boiling. Place green beans in wire strainer; lower into boiling water. Cover and cook 5 minutes. Immediately rinse under running cold water; drain.

Place beans, jícama and bell peppers in separate bowls. Pour ¼ cup Herbed Vinaigrette over each vegetable. Cover and refrigerate at least 1 hour.

Arrange beans, jícama and bell peppers on lettuce leaves in Mexican flag design. Place olives in center of rectangle formed by jícama.

6 TO 8 SERVINGS

HERBED VINAIGRETTE

½ cup olive or vegetable oil
2 tablespoons lemon juice
2 tablespoons lime juice
1 tablespoon wine vinegar
1 teaspoon snipped parsley
1 teaspoon chile powder
½ teaspoon dry mustard
¼ teaspoon salt
¼ teaspoon dried basil leaves
¼ teaspoon dried oregano leaves
¼ teaspoon ground sage
⅛ teaspoon freshly ground pepper
1 clove garlic, finely chopped

Shake all ingredients in tightly covered container.

Mexican Flag Salad

Jícama Citrus Salad with Sangria Dressing

3 large oranges, pared and sectioned
2 red grapefruit, pared and sectioned
1 medium jícama (about 1 pound), pared and cut into
  ¹/₂-inch cubes
Sangria Dressing (below)

Arrange oranges, grapefruit and jícama on 8 salad plates or mix together. Serve with Sangria Dressing.

8 SERVINGS

SANGRIA DRESSING

¹/₄ cup vegetable oil
¹/₄ cup dry red wine
2 tablespoons honey
2 tablespoons orange juice

Shake all ingredients in tightly covered container.

Orange Salad with Pecan Dressing

4 oranges, pared
1 head lettuce, torn into bite-size pieces
Pecan Dressing (below)

Cut oranges crosswise into slices; cut slices into fourths. Mix oranges and lettuce. Toss with Pecan Dressing.

6 SERVINGS

PECAN DRESSING

¹/₄ cup ground pecans
2 tablespoons mayonnaise or salad dressing
2 tablespoons dairy sour cream
1 tablespoon lime juice
¹/₂ teaspoon sugar
¹/₂ teaspoon salt
¹/₈ teaspoon ground cinnamon
Dash of pepper

Mix all ingredients.

Jícama Citrus Salad with Sangria Dressing

Rio Grande Melon Salad

2 cups watermelon balls
2 mangoes or papayas, pared and sliced
1/2 honeydew melon, pared, seeded and thinly sliced
3/4 cup seedless red grape halves
1 large bunch watercress
Honey-Lime Dressing (below)

Arrange fruits on watercress. Drizzle with Honey-Lime Dressing.

6 SERVINGS

HONEY-LIME DRESSING

1/3 cup vegetable oil
1/4 teaspoon grated lime peel
2 tablespoons lime juice
1 tablespoon honey

Shake all ingredients in tightly covered container.

Stuffed Red Chiles

6 red Anaheim chiles or 3 red bell peppers
1 large onion, finely chopped (about 1 cup)
1 serrano chile, seeded and finely chopped
1 clove garlic, finely chopped
2 tablespoons vegetable oil
1 cup whole kernel corn
1 cup shredded Chihuahua or Monterey Jack cheese (4 ounces)
1/2 cup dairy sour cream
Fresh cilantro leaves

Heat oven to 375°. Cut Anaheim chiles lengthwise into halves; remove seeds. Cook onion, serrano chile and garlic in oil in 10-inch skillet until onion is tender. Stir in corn, shredded cheese and sour cream.

Fill each chile half with cheese mixture; place in ungreased rectangular pan, 13 x 9 x 2 inches. Cover and bake until crisp-tender, chiles about 25 minutes, bell peppers about 35 minutes. Garnish with cilantro leaves.

6 SERVINGS

Spicy Baked Cauliflower

1 medium head cauliflower (about 2 pounds), separated into flowerets
1 medium onion, chopped (about 1/2 cup)
2 tablespoons vegetable oil
1 medium green bell pepper, chopped
1 large tomato, chopped (about 1 cup)
1 jalapeño chile, seeded and finely chopped
1 clove garlic, finely chopped
1 tablespoon coarsely chopped green olives
1 tablespoon snipped parsley
1 teaspoon capers
1/2 teaspoon salt
1/4 cup dry bread crumbs
1/2 cup shredded Cheddar cheese (2 ounces)

Heat oven to 350°. Heat 1 inch salted water (1/2 teaspoon salt to 1 cup water) to boiling. Add cauliflower. Cover and boil 5 minutes; drain. Arrange cauliflower in ungreased rectangular baking dish, 10 x 6 x 1 1/2 inches.

Cook and stir onion in oil in 10-inch skillet until tender. Stir in remaining ingredients except bread crumbs and cheese; cook uncovered 5 minutes. Spoon over cauliflower. Sprinkle with bread crumbs and cheese. Bake uncovered until cheese is melted, about 15 minutes.

5 SERVINGS

Rio Grande Melon Salad

Cinnamon Squash Rings

2 tablespoons packed brown sugar
2 tablespoons milk
1 egg
¾ cup soft bread crumbs (about 2½ slices bread)
¼ cup yellow or white cornmeal
2 teaspoons ground cinnamon
1 large acorn squash (about 1½ pounds), cut crosswise
    into ½-inch slices and seeded
⅓ cup margarine or butter, melted

Heat oven to 400°. Mix brown sugar, milk and egg. Mix bread crumbs, cornmeal and cinnamon. Dip squash slices into egg mixture, and coat with bread crumb mixture; repeat.

Place in ungreased rectangular pan, 13 x 9 x 2 inches; drizzle with margarine. Bake uncovered until squash is tender, 30 to 35 minutes.

6 SERVINGS

Baked Chayotes with Tomatoes

4 medium chayotes
2 slices bacon, cut into ½-inch pieces
2 tablespoons vegetable oil
½ teaspoon salt
½ teaspoon dried oregano leaves
¼ teaspoon ground nutmeg
¼ teaspoon pepper
4 medium tomatoes, chopped (about 4 cups)
1 large onion, chopped (about 1 cup)
1 clove garlic, finely chopped
1 cup shredded Monterey Jack cheese (4 ounces)

Pare chayotes; cut lengthwise into fourths. Remove seeds. Heat enough salted water to cover chayotes (½ teaspoon salt to 1 cup water) to boiling. Add chayotes. Cover and boil until crisp-tender, 15 to 20 minutes; drain. Arrange chayotes in ungreased rectangular baking dish, 13 x 9 x 2 inches.

Cook and stir bacon in 2-quart saucepan until crisp. Stir in remaining ingredients except cheese. Heat to boiling; reduce heat. Simmer uncovered 15 minutes.

Heat oven to 350°. Pour vegetable mixture over chayotes; sprinkle with cheese. Bake uncovered until hot and bubbly and cheese is melted, about 15 minutes.

8 SERVINGS

Spinach Budín

A budín ("pudding") is a popular way to prepare vegetables in the Southwest. Budín denotes a soufflélike dish, frequently made with spinach, zucchini or carrots.

2 poblano chiles, roasted, peeled (page 15), seeded and
    chopped
1 medium onion, finely chopped (about ½ cup)
2 packages (10 ounces each) frozen chopped spinach,
    thawed and drained
2 tablespoons margarine or butter
½ cup half-and-half
½ cup tomato sauce
¼ teaspoon salt
3 eggs, separated
¼ cup finely shredded Monterey Jack cheese (2 ounces)

Heat oven to 350°. Cook and stir chiles, onion and spinach in margarine in 10-inch skillet until onion is tender. Stir in half-and-half, tomato sauce and salt.

Beat egg whites in large bowl until stiff. Beat egg yolks in small bowl until thick and lemon colored; stir into spinach mixture. Fold egg whites into spinach mixture.

Carefully pour into greased 2-quart soufflé dish. Bake until knife inserted in center comes out clean, about 30 minutes. Sprinkle with cheese.

6 SERVINGS

Cinnamon Squash Rings

Mustard Artichoke Hearts

1 small onion, chopped (about ¼ cup)
2 tablespoons margarine or butter
2 tablespoons brandy
1 tablespoon prepared mustard
½ teaspoon ground cumin
¼ teaspoon salt
⅛ teaspoon pepper
1 clove garlic, finely chopped
2 cans (14 ounces each) artichoke hearts, drained and
   cut into halves
¼ cup snipped parsley

Cook and stir onion in margarine in 10-inch skillet over medium heat until tender. Stir in brandy; simmer uncovered 2 minutes.

Stir in remaining ingredients except artichoke hearts and parsley. Stir in artichoke hearts; cook uncovered 5 minutes, stirring occasionally. Stir in parsley.

6 SERVINGS

Wilted Spinach

Fresh, lightly cooked spinach is a treat. Nutmeg is a heady, traditional seasoning for spinach, here tossed briefly in hot bacon fat.

1 medium onion, chopped (about ½ cup)
1 slice bacon, cut up
1 clove garlic, finely chopped
2 tablespoons margarine or butter
2 tablespoons olive or vegetable oil
½ teaspoon salt
¼ teaspoon pepper
¼ teaspoon ground nutmeg
1 pound fresh spinach
2 tablespoons lime juice

Cook and stir onion, bacon and garlic in margarine and oil in 4-quart Dutch oven over medium heat until bacon is crisp; reduce heat. Stir in salt, pepper and nutmeg. Add spinach; toss just until spinach is wilted. Drizzle with lime juice.

6 SERVINGS

Southwest Vegetable Sauté

Lime Butter Sauce (page 29)
1 medium onion, finely chopped (about ½ cup)
2 cloves garlic, finely chopped
¼ cup margarine or butter
4 very small pattypan squash (about 4 ounces each),
   cut into halves
2 small zucchini, cut into ¼-inch strips
2 small yellow squash, cut into ¼-inch strips
1 medium chayote, pared, seeded and cut into ½-inch
   cubes
1 small red bell pepper, cut into thin rings
1 small yellow bell pepper, cut into thin rings
½ teaspoon salt
¼ teaspoon ground red pepper
8 fresh squash blossoms, if desired

Prepare Lime Butter Sauce; reserve. Cook and stir onion and garlic in margarine in 4-quart Dutch oven until onion is tender.

Stir in remaining ingredients except squash blossoms. Cook over medium heat, stirring occasionally, until vegetables are crisp-tender; stir in squash blossoms. Serve with Lime Butter Sauce.

8 SERVINGS

Adobe Bread

This crusty bread of the Pueblo Indians is still baked today in beehive-shaped ovens called *hornos*. Often the round loaves of the Indians are decorated with symbols (bear paws or squash blossoms, for example) for special occasions. Authentic Pueblo bread can't be duplicated in ordinary ovens; the *horno* bakes the bread with heat that slowly decreases as the wood fire dies.

2 cups whole wheat flour
¼ cup sugar
¼ cup shortening or lard
2 teaspoons salt
2 packages active dry yeast
2 cups very warm water (120° to 130°)
3 to 4 cups all-purpose flour
2 teaspoons all-purpose flour

Mix whole wheat flour, sugar, shortening, salt and yeast in large bowl; stir in warm water. Beat on low speed 1 minute, scraping bowl frequently. Beat on medium speed 1 minute, scraping bowl frequently. Stir in enough all-purpose flour, 1 cup at a time, to make dough easy to handle.

Turn dough onto lightly floured surface; knead until smooth and elastic, about 10 minutes. Place in greased medium bowl; turn greased side up. Cover and let rise in warm place until double, 40 to 60 minutes. (Dough is ready if indentation remains when dough is touched.)

Punch down dough; divide into halves. Let rest 5 minutes. Shape each half into a round, slightly flat loaf. Place loaves on opposite corners of greased large cookie sheet. Cover and let rise until double, 40 to 50 minutes.

Heat oven to 375°. Make ½-inch-deep slashes across top of each loaf in lattice design. Sprinkle each loaf with 1 teaspoon all-purpose flour. Bake until loaves are deep golden brown and sound hollow when tapped, 35 to 40 minutes. Cool on wire rack.

2 LOAVES

Adobe Bread

Vegetable Cornmeal Muffins

1¼ cups yellow cornmeal
¾ cup all-purpose flour
¼ cup shortening
1½ cups buttermilk
2 teaspoons baking powder
1 teaspoon sugar
1 teaspoon salt
½ teaspoon baking soda
2 eggs
1 cup shredded zucchini, drained
½ cup chopped red bell pepper
2 tablespoons chopped jalapeño or serrano chiles

Heat oven to 450°. Grease 16 medium muffin cups, 2½ x 1¼ inches, or line muffin cups with paper baking cups.

Mix all ingredients except zucchini, bell pepper and chiles; beat vigorously 30 seconds. Stir in remaining ingredients.

Fill muffin cups about ⅞ full. Bake until light golden brown, 20 to 25 minutes. Remove from pan immediately.

16 MUFFINS

Desserts and Sweets

Southwestern desserts reflect the region's Mexican and Indian heritage. They are quite sweet and very substantial. Puddings, custards, deep-fried pastries and pralines are favorites. Fresh fruit is the original Mexican dessert, a refreshing finale to a spicy meal. "New" southwestern desserts are often wildly innovative, inspired by local color and motifs.

Southwest Lemon Fruit Tart

Southwest Lemon Fruit Tart

A soothing pecan crust filled with lemon mousse and topped with fresh fruit: a perfect contrast to a spicy southwestern meal. This is a beautiful tart, sensational with its glistening arrangement of different fruits. It would be an elegant finish to any dinner party.

Pecan Crust (below)
1 teaspoon unflavored gelatin
1 tablespoon cold water
1/2 cup sugar
2 eggs
2 tablespoons grated lemon peel
1/4 cup lemon juice
1/2 cup whipping cream
1 cup strawberry halves
1 cup raspberries
1/2 cup blackberries or blueberries
1 mango or papaya, pared and sliced
1/3 cup guava jelly or apricot jam, melted

Prepare Pecan Crust; cool. Sprinkle gelatin on cold water in 1 1/2-quart saucepan to soften. Beat sugar and eggs until thick and lemon colored; stir into gelatin mixture. Heat just to boiling over low heat, stirring constantly, about 15 minutes. Remove from heat; stir in lemon peel and juice.

Beat whipping cream in chilled medium bowl until soft peaks form. Fold in lemon mixture; pour into Pecan Crust. Refrigerate 2 hours. Arrange fruits on top; drizzle with jelly. Refrigerate any remaining tart.

8 SERVINGS

PECAN CRUST

1 cup all-purpose flour
1/2 cup finely chopped pecans
1/4 cup sugar
1/4 cup margarine or butter, softened
1 egg

Heat oven to 375°. Mix flour, pecans and sugar; mix in margarine and egg until crumbly. Press in bottom and up side of greased tart pan, 9 x 1 inch. Bake until light golden brown, 15 to 20 minutes.

Date-Pecan Upside-down Cake

1/4 cup plus 2 tablespoons margarine or butter
2/3 cup packed brown sugar
12 pitted dates
1 cup coarsely chopped pecans
1 cup all-purpose flour
3/4 cup granulated sugar
1/3 cup shortening
3/4 cup milk
1 1/2 teaspoons baking powder
1 teaspoon vanilla
1/2 teaspoon salt
1 egg
Whipped cream

Heat oven to 350°. Heat margarine in 10-inch ovenproof skillet or square pan, 9 x 9 x 2 inches, in oven until melted. Sprinkle evenly with brown sugar. Arrange dates on top so that each serving will include one date; sprinkle with pecans.

Beat remaining ingredients except whipped cream in large bowl on low speed, scraping bowl constantly, 30 seconds. Beat on high speed, scraping bowl occasionally, 3 minutes. Pour evenly over dates and pecans.

Bake until wooden pick inserted in center comes out clean, 40 to 45 minutes. Loosen edge of cake with knife. Invert on heatproof platter; leave skillet over cake a few minutes. Serve warm with whipped cream.

12 SERVINGS

Date-Pecan Upside-down Cake

Tucson Lemon Cake

Lemon cakes are very popular in Arizona, thanks to the profusion of local lemon groves. This lemony cake is dramatically shot through with poppy seeds. A lemon glaze soaks into the cake while it is still hot from the oven.

1½ cups sugar
½ cup margarine or butter, softened
3 eggs
2½ cups all-purpose flour
1 teaspoon baking soda
½ teaspoon salt
1 cup buttermilk
¼ cup poppy seed
2 tablespoons grated lemon peel
2 tablespoons lemon juice
Lemon Glaze (below)

Heat oven to 325°. Grease and flour 12-cup bundt cake pan or tube pan, 10 x 4 inches. Beat sugar and margarine in large bowl on medium speed until light and fluffy. Beat in eggs, 1 at a time.

Mix flour, baking soda and salt; beat into sugar mixture alternately with buttermilk until well blended. Stir in poppy seed, lemon peel and lemon juice. Spread in pan.

Bake until wooden pick inserted in center comes out clean, 50 to 55 minutes. Immediately poke holes in top of cake with long-tined fork; pour about ⅔ of the Lemon Glaze over top. Cool 20 minutes. Invert on heatproof serving plate; remove pan. Spread with remaining glaze.

16 SERVINGS

LEMON GLAZE

2 cups powdered sugar
¼ cup margarine or butter, melted
2 tablespoons grated lemon peel
¼ cup lemon juice

Mix all ingredients.

Tucson Lemon Cake

Toasted Almond Pound Cake

2¾ cups sugar
1¼ cups margarine or butter
5 eggs
3 cups all-purpose flour
2 teaspoons ground cinnamon
1 teaspoon baking powder
¼ teaspoon salt
1 cup evaporated milk
1½ cups chopped blanched almonds, toasted
Cinnamon-Chocolate Sauce (below)
Whipped cream

Heat oven to 350°. Grease and flour 12-cup bundt cake pan or tube pan, 10 x 4 inches. Beat sugar, margarine and eggs in large bowl on low speed, scraping bowl constantly, 30 seconds. Beat batter on high speed, scraping bowl occasionally, 5 minutes.

Beat in flour, cinnamon, baking powder and salt alternately with milk, on low speed. Fold in almonds. Spread in pan.

Bake until wooden pick inserted in center comes out clean, 70 to 80 minutes. Cool 20 minutes. Invert on heatproof serving plate; remove pan. Serve with Cinnamon-Chocolate Sauce and whipped cream.

16 SERVINGS

CINNAMON-CHOCOLATE SAUCE

1 cup whipping cream
½ cup sugar
3 ounces unsweetened chocolate
1 tablespoon margarine or butter
1 teaspoon ground cinnamon

Heat whipping cream, sugar and chocolate to boiling over medium heat, stirring constantly. Boil and stir until chocolate is well blended, about 30 seconds. Remove from heat; stir in margarine and cinnamon.

Mango Mousse

½ cup sugar
2 envelopes unflavored gelatin
4 eggs
3 egg yolks
2 cups mashed ripe mangoes (about 3 mangoes)
¼ cup brandy
¼ teaspoon almond extract
2 cups whipping cream
Sweetened whipped cream

Mix sugar and gelatin in 2-quart saucepan. Beat eggs and egg yolks until thick and lemon colored, about 5 minutes.

Stir eggs into gelatin mixture. Heat just to boiling over medium heat, stirring constantly. Remove from heat; stir in mangoes, brandy and almond extract. Refrigerate just until gelatin mixture mounds slightly when dropped from a spoon, about 1½ hours.

Beat whipping cream in chilled bowl until stiff. Fold mango mixture into whipped cream. Pour into 8-cup mold. Refrigerate until firm, about 4 hours; unmold. Serve with sweetened whipped cream. Garnish with mango slices if desired.

12 SERVINGS

Apricot Mousse: Substitute 1 can (30 ounces) apricot halves, drained, for the mangoes. Place apricots in blender container; cover and blend on high speed until smooth, about 1 minute. Decrease sugar to ¼ cup.

Peach Mousse: Substitute 1 can (29 ounces) sliced peaches, drained, for the mangoes. Place peaches in blender container; cover and blend on high speed until smooth, about 1 minute. Decrease sugar to ¼ cup.

Natillas

Natillas

Natillas are a southwestern version of floating island: little meringues set adrift on a pool of thin custard. Just before serving, run the dessert under the broiler for a pretty, golden effect.

4 eggs, separated
½ teaspoon cream of tartar
1 cup granulated sugar
4 cups milk
½ cup granulated sugar
1 teaspoon vanilla
¼ teaspoon salt
⅛ teaspoon ground cinnamon
Powdered sugar, sifted

Beat egg whites and cream of tartar in small bowl until foamy. Beat in 1 cup granulated sugar, 1 tablespoon at a time; continue beating until stiff and glossy. Do not underbeat.

Heat milk to simmering in 10-inch skillet over medium heat; reduce heat just until bubbles form around edge of skillet. Drop 12 mounds of egg white mixture, 3 or 4 at a time, into hot milk. Cook uncovered 2 minutes; turn gently. Cook uncovered 2 minutes longer. Remove meringues with slotted spoon and drain.

Strain milk; reserve 2¼ cups. Mix egg yolks, ½ cup granulated sugar, the vanilla, salt and cinnamon in heavy 2-quart nonaluminum saucepan.

Gradually stir in reserved milk. Cook over low heat, stirring constantly, until mixture coats a metal spoon, about 20 minutes. Remove from heat; place saucepan in cold water, stirring occasionally, until cool.

Place meringues in shallow 3-quart nonaluminum casserole. Pour custard over meringues; refrigerate 1 hour.

Just before serving, set oven control to broil. Sprinkle custard and meringues with powdered sugar. Broil with tops of meringues about 4 inches from heat until light brown, about 2 minutes. Refrigerate any remaining dessert.

6 SERVINGS

Mexican Sweet Buns

Sweet-topped buns, or *conchas*, are named for the seashell design drawn in the flavored topping. Mexican bakers use a small metal cutter to stamp the design into the topping, but the pattern is easily drawn freehand with a knife.

1 package regular active dry yeast
½ cup warm water (105° to 115°)
½ cup lukewarm milk (scalded then cooled)
⅓ cup sugar
⅓ cup margarine or butter, softened
1 teaspoon salt
1 egg
3½ to 4 cups all-purpose flour
Flavored Topping Dough (right)

Dissolve yeast in warm water in large bowl. Stir in milk, sugar, margarine, salt, egg and 2 cups of the flour. Beat until smooth. Stir in enough remaining flour to make dough easy to handle.

Turn onto lightly floured surface; knead until smooth and elastic, about 5 minutes. Place in greased large bowl; turn greased side up. Cover and let rise in warm place until double, about 1½ hours. (Dough is ready if indentation remains when touched.)

Prepare Flavored Topping Dough; cover with plastic wrap to prevent from drying. Punch down sweet bun dough. Divide into 12 equal pieces; shape each piece into ball. Place on greased cookie sheet. Divide each part topping dough into 4 equal pieces. Pat each piece into 3-inch circle. Place 1 circle on each ball of dough, shaping down over ball. Make 5 or 6 cuts across topping, using a table knife, to form a shell pattern. Cover and let rise until double, about 40 minutes.

Heat oven to 375°. Bake until golden brown, about 20 minutes.

1 DOZEN ROLLS

FLAVORED TOPPING DOUGH

⅓ cup sugar
¼ cup margarine or butter
½ cup all-purpose flour
1 teaspoon ground cinnamon
¼ teaspoon vanilla
1½ teaspoons grated orange peel

Beat sugar and margarine until light and fluffy. Stir in flour until mixture is consistency of thick paste. Divide into 3 equal parts. Stir cinnamon into one part, vanilla into one part and orange peel into one part.

Place 1 circle of topping on each ball of dough, shaping down over ball.

Make 5 or 6 cuts across topping, using table knife, to form shell pattern.

New Mexico Piñon Candy

2 cones piloncillo, shredded (about 1¼ cups), or 1 cup
  packed dark brown sugar
1 cup water
2 tablespoons butter*
1½ cups toasted pine nuts or pecan halves (page 19)
1 teaspoon vanilla

Heat piloncillo and water to boiling in 2-quart saucepan, stirring constantly; reduce heat slightly. Cook, without stirring, to 236° on candy thermometer or until small amount of mixture dropped into very cold water forms a soft ball that flattens when removed from water; remove from heat. Immediately remove thermometer; stir in butter. Cool 8 minutes without stirring.

Stir in pine nuts and vanilla. Beat with spoon until slightly thickened and mixture just coats pine nuts but remains glossy, about 1 minute. Drop by rounded teaspoonfuls onto waxed paper. Let stand until candies are firm. Store tightly covered at room temperature.

ABOUT 24 CANDIES

* Margarine not recommended.

New Mexico Biscochitos

Biscochitos are Mexico's answer to the Old World seed cookie. Rich with the flavor of anise, these holiday cookies were cut into *fleur de lis* shapes for Christmas. *Biscochitos* are quite short—traditionally a high ratio of lard to flour and sugar—and are as easy to roll out and cut as sugar cookies. Biscochitos are the official state cookie of New Mexico.

1 cup sugar
1 cup margarine or butter, softened
3 tablespoons sweet sherry
1 egg
3 cups all-purpose flour
2 teaspoons baking powder
2 teaspoons anise seed, crushed
¼ teaspoon salt
¼ cup sugar
1 teaspoon ground cinnamon

Heat oven to 350°. Mix sugar, margarine, sherry and egg in large bowl. Stir in remaining ingredients except ¼ cup sugar and the cinnamon. Divide dough into halves. Roll each half ¼ inch thick on lightly floured board.

Cut into desired shapes with cookie cutters; place on ungreased cookie sheet. Mix ¼ cup sugar and the cinnamon; sprinkle on cookies. Bake until light golden brown, 10 to 12 minutes.

ABOUT 4 DOZEN 2-INCH COOKIES

New Mexico Biscochitos and New Mexico Piñon Candy

Beans
Pinto Beans

Refried Beans

Vegetables
Southwest Vegetable Sauté

Tortillas
Flour Tortillas

Used In
Bean and Garlic Dip
Refried Beans

Beef Burritos
Filled Tortillas
Green Enchiladas
Mixed Tostadas
Red Enchiladas

Used In
Grilled Red Snapper with Vegetable Sauté

Used In
Filled Tortillas

Index

GENERAL MILLS, INC.

Editor: Karen Couné
Associate Food Editor: Julie H. Turnbull
Test Kitchen Home Economist: Mary Hallin Johnson
Recipe Copy Editor: Lauren Long
Administrative Assistant: Phyllis Weinbender
Food Stylists: Cindy Lund, Katie W. McElroy, Mary Sethre
Photographer: Nanci E. Doonan
Photography Assistant: Carolyn Luxmoore
Director, Betty Crocker Food and Publications Center: Marcia Copeland
Assistant Manager, Publications: Lois Tlusty

PRENTICE HALL

Vice President and Associate Publisher: Anne Zeman
Senior Editor: Rebecca W. Atwater
Creative Director: J. C. Suarès
Designers: Patricia Fabricant, Fred Latasa, Christina Sun
Prop Stylist: Janice Ervin

Many of the plates featured in *Betty Crocker's Southwest Cooking* were commissioned especially for this book. Artists: Nina Duran (front cover, pages 23, 33, 83, 95, 105, 114, 200–201); Patricia Fabricant (page 79); Jillene Kingstedt (pages 4, 121, 133); Tomar Levine (pages 77, 97, 123, 124, 129, 155, 177, 195); Helène Maumy-Florescu (pages 69, 80, 131); J. C. Suarès (pages 51, 137, 150, 167); Christina Sun (pages 54, 109, 149); and Ardith Truhan (back cover, pages 86–87, 88, 99, 116, 144, 171).